THE

WILDERNESS ROAD

A DESCRIPTION OF THE

ROUTES OF TRAVEL

BY WHICH THE PIONEERS AND EARLY SETTLERS FIRST
CAME TO KENTUCKY

PREPARED FOR

THE FILSON CLUB

BY

THOMAS SPEED

Southernw Historical Press, Inc.
Greenville, South Carolina

This volume was reproduced
from a personal copy located in
the Publishers private library

Please direct all correspondence and book orders to:
SOUTHERN HISTORICAL PRESS, Inc.
PO Box 1267
Greenville, SC   29602-1267

Originally printed: New York, NY 1886
ISBN #978-1-63914-146-3
Printed in the United States of America

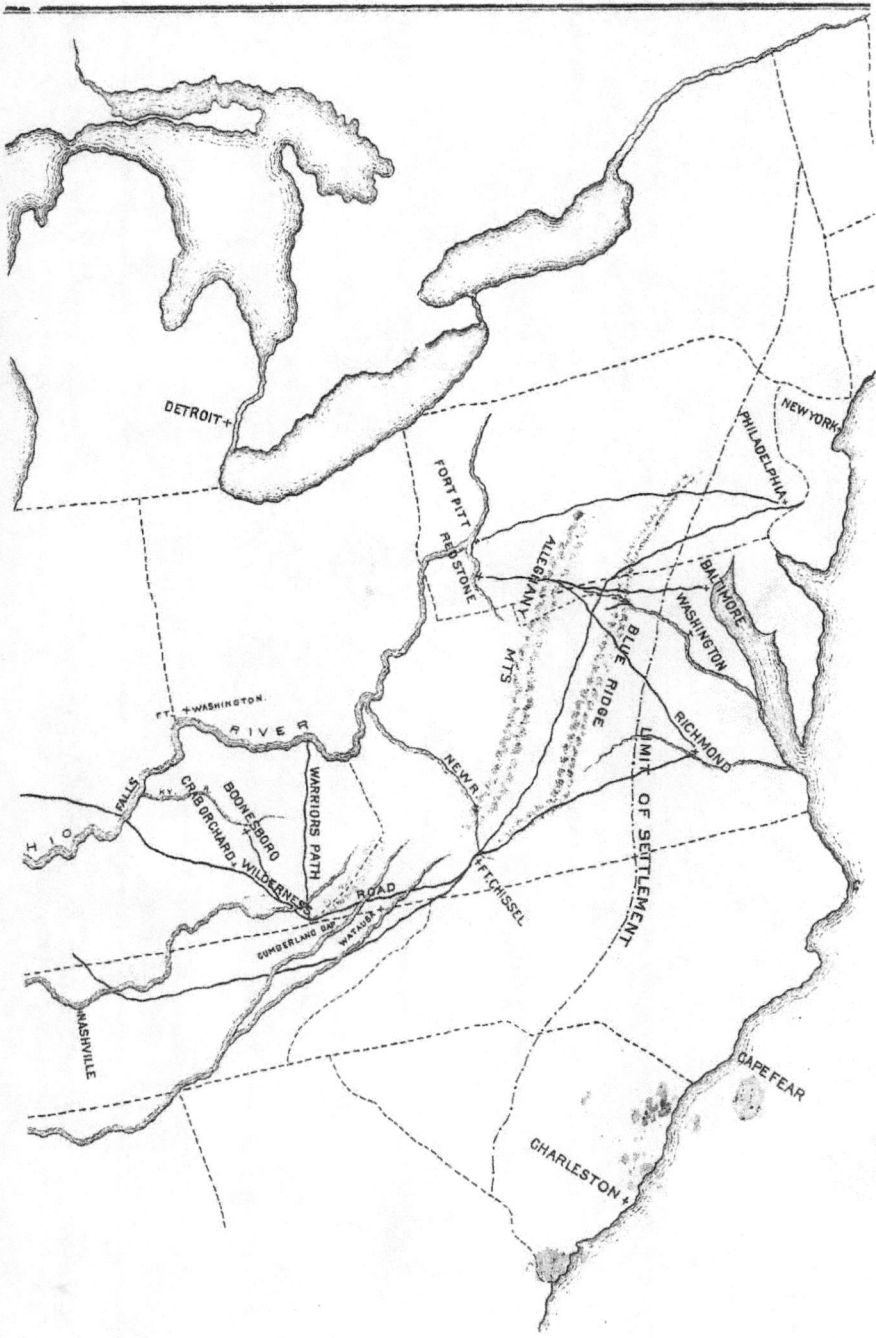

PREFACE.

The story of the remarkable immigration to Kentucky which commenced in 1775, and in less than twenty years created a State in the Western wilderness with a population of nearly one hundred thousand, is more traditional than historical.

Many are now living, among our older citizens, who remember how their fathers and mothers told them of their travel to Kentucky from Virginia, or the Carolinas, or Maryland, or Pennsylvania. The greater portion of this travel in the early days was over the old Wilderness Road, though many persons made their way down the Ohio.

No attempt has been made to gather up the fragmentary accounts of this travel in the form of an historic narrative.

The account herewith presented, was prepared for the Filson Club, and is published by its direction for the purpose of preserving the facts and incidents it contains, and in the hope that it will stimulate further research and the production of additional historic material pertaining to the early Kentucky annals.

LOUISVILLE, KY., December 30, 1885.

The Wilderness Road.

———————

Before the invention of steamboats and railroads the populations of the world fringed the sea-coasts or followed navigable streams into the interior. The settlement of America was no exception to this rule; the colonists clung tenaciously to the sea over which they came from the mother country. Less than two hundred miles inland, and parallel with the Atlantic coast were the mountains. Beyond these lay a wilderness of unknown extent, the occupation of which presented obstacles scarcely less formidable than those which attended the first planting of the colonies. The colonists made no attempt at such occupation until the last quarter of the last century. They were content, for a period of one hundred and fifty years, with possessions immediately along the coast. Up to the close of the Revolutionary war the three millions of people who had "engaged in the holy cause of liberty" only knew the country east of the Alleghany Mountains, and of this they only occupied so much as lay within one hundred miles or less of the sea. It is remarkable how slowly the New

World was settled after its discovery. From 1492 until the planting of the first colony at Jamestown was more than an entire century, and then for a century and a half more no impression was made upon the continent other than was shown in the fringe of settlements along the Atlantic border. At the time the colonists had fully achieved their independence a singularly small extent of the States of New York, Pennsylvania, Virginia, and the Carolinas had been settled. The outposts of civilization in those States were not in the western but in the eastern parts. The Indians roamed in undisputed freedom over nearly all of New York west of the Hudson. The massacre at Wyoming, in 1778, took place less than one hundred miles west of New York City, at what was then a frontier village of Pennsylvania. The greater portion of Virginia and the Carolinas was an unbroken solitude, the hunting ground of savages, and the hiding place of wild beasts.

Fort Pitt was a distant outpost—merely a foothold in the far West. Another weak settlement had taken root on the head waters of the Holston River, near where is now the line between Virginia and Tennessee; it was known as the Watauga settlement. But no real impression was made upon the great West until after the war of the Revolution. With the accomplishment of independence, however, the time came for passing the western barriers; the section of occupied territory was to widen from a narrow ribbon along the coast line to the whole extent of the continent. Space was to be cleared for the gigantic growth of the new

Republic, and the coming wonders of the railway and steam navigation.

It was in the far-distant region of Kentucky that the permanent occupation of the West began. In the heart of that region, full five hundred miles as the crow flies from the sea-coast, and more than three hundred miles beyond the crests of the mountains, population suddenly gathered and civilization suddenly bloomed.

A glance at the map shows the immense distance this Kentucky civilization was from that of the East. It grew up in the wilderness, while another wilderness three hundred miles in extent separated it from the nearest inhabited country. In 1790 Kentucky had a population of over 73,-000. Even at that date no growth westward had been made in New York State, and scarcely any had been made in Pennsylvania. But little extension of settlements had been made in Virginia, and the borders of the present State of Ohio had only been here and there touched. In two more years Kentucky took her position in the Union as a State. In 1800 her population was 220,000, being then nearly as great as that of Connecticut; only one third less than that of Maryland; more than half that of Massachusetts; more than one third that of Pennsylvania; one fourth that of Virginia, and nearly one fourth that of the two Carolinas.

These facts show not only how immigration went westward into Kentucky in advance of any other point, but also that it went by a mighty leap over and beyond the barriers. It was not the extension of continuously occupied country like a peninsula of civilization stretching into the regions of the West; it was rather like an island of population far away from shore, only to be reached by a long, rough, and perilous passage.

The rapid growth of this Western plant is also suggested. In the short space of twenty years Kentucky took rank and station with the Atlantic States which were founded one hundred and fifty years before. It would be interesting to study the causes of these remarkable facts; among them may be mentioned the glowing accounts of the fertility and beauty of the "Land of Kentucke," spread by the early explorers; the easy terms on which the lands might be obtained, and the privilege of paying for them in the depreciated colonial and continental paper money; the high taxes, distress, and dissatisfaction following the Revolutionary war; the populousness of the States directly east of Kentucky, which had the effect to start the westward movement at that point; the important fact that the Kentucky lands were not occupied by any of the Indian tribes as a place of residence, which rendered their appropriation by the whites less difficult than it would otherwise have been. Kentucky was the hunting ground of the Indians, whose villages and towns were north of the Ohio, and of the Cherokees and Chickasaws of the South. It is true the pioneers encountered fierce Indian hostilities, for the savages were jealous of the occupation of their hunting ground; but they might have found a fiercer opposition if Kentucky, like Ohio and New York, had been the actual residence of warlike tribes.

But notwithstanding all the inducements and advantages, the settlement of Kentucky was a most remarkable event. It is a wonderful fact, as we now look back upon it, that thousands of families left their "peaceable habitations," as Boone expresses it, "to wander through the wilderness of America in quest of the country of Kentucky." It was not an adventure of bold men alone, but a movement of men, women, and children. It is equally wonderful that from the first they were imbued with the idea of permanent settlement and residence in that far-west country. It was to be their home; return was not thought of. They carried with them all their possessions, and as the altar-fire for the distant colony they carried with them a clear perception of the prime necessity of stable government, of obedience to law, and the observance of order. This led to the speedy establishment of the State, and its admission into the Union less than twenty years from the time the immigration began.

Much interest attaches to the ways of travel over which these immigrants came. Through the great wilderness a vast concourse made its way. But the direction, character, and features of the roads is but little understood. There is no description in existence showing them as they appeared when alive with western movers. It is only by reference to numerous authorities, many of them rare and difficult to procure, that any account can be obtained. Many interesting facts are found in the almost illegible manuscript of old letters, journals, and diaries, and many exist only in traditional form.

The object of this paper is to gather together such information as can be obtained touching these old highways; to give their courses and distances; to show by whom they were laid out and traversed, and present some idea of the incidents, difficulties, and dangers of early travel.

Captain Imlay, an officer in the Revolutionary war, who wrote from personal observation, and whose book was first published in 1792, gave a brief account of the courses of travel from the East to Kentucky. From him we get a very distinct statement of two routes of travel; the one down the Ohio River, the other "through the great wilderness," by way of Cumberland Gap.

He says travelers from the more northerly States passed along a road which ran out from Philadelphia, through the upper and central points of Pennsylvania to Pittsburgh, and from thence made their way down the Ohio River. South of this Pennsylvania road another led out from Baltimore, passing Old Town and Cumberland Fort on the Potomac River, and along Braddock's road to Redstone Old Fort (now Brownsville), on the Monongahela River, sixty miles above its mouth. From that point travelers also made their way to Kentucky by water. This lower road subsequently became the celebrated National turnpike or Cumberland road, the general Government having improved it and made it a post-road, and a great connecting link between the East and West.

According to Imlay travelers found tolerable accommodations along each of these roads as far west as Pittsburgh. The way over the mountains, he says, was somewhat rough, but not difficult to pass. But he wrote eighteen years after the great immigration to Kentucky first commenced, and at a time when Kentucky was a State with nearly 100,000 inhabitants. Even then, he says, the way from Pittsburgh by river was so tedious and dangerous that those who did not carry much baggage found the way "through the great wilderness" preferable. The westward-bound movers, who were burdened with household stuff and a few implements for farming, could wagon their luggage out from Philadelphia or Baltimore or other eastern points to Pittsburgh or to Redstone Old Fort on the Monongahela in about twenty days. Imlay says the wagon might be covered with canvas, and so afford a place to sleep at night; also by having camp-kettles food could be prepared when the evening halt was made by some stream, while the horses were fed with the provender carried along. This manner of journeying, he says, was not disagreeable, but in a fine season extremely pleasant. He recommended the season of autumn as the most eligible for the trip, as the roads were drier, and provisions and forage more plentiful than at any other time.

Even as late as 1792, when Imlay wrote, there was no such convenience as a regular business of carrying passengers and their luggage down the Ohio, but at Pittsburgh or

Old Fort a flat-boat or passenger boat might be obtained, according to the good luck of the traveler.

Accepting the statement of Imlay as true, that travelers without much baggage found the best and most expeditious way to Kentucky to be through the wilderness, it shows most strikingly what labors, difficulties, and perils had to be encountered on the western journey, when the traveler from points as high north as Philadelphia found the most available route was through the mountains of Virginia, by way of Cumberland Gap, and through the mountains of Eastern Kentucky.

The distance from Philadelphia to the interior of Kentucky by way of Cumberland Gap was nearly eight hundred miles. The line of travel was through Lancaster, Yorktown, and Abbottstown to the Potomac River at Wadkin's Ferry; thence through Martinsburg and Winchester, up the Shenandoah Valley through Staunton, and, following the great trough between the mountain ranges, it passed over the high ground known as the "divide:" there it left the waters which "run toward sunrise," and reached an important station at the waters of New River, which run to the west. At that point another road, which led out from Richmond through the central parts of Virginia, intersected or rather came into the one just described. Thus were brought together two tides of immigrants. Near the "forks of the road" stood Fort Chissel, a rude block-house, built in 1758 by Colonel Bird immediately after the British and Americans captured Fort Duquesne from the French, and called it Fort Pitt. Fort Chissel was intended as a menace to the Cherokee Indians; it was an outpost in the wilderness of the West, yet from the point where it stood to Cumberland Gap was nearly two hundred miles. It is a point of great interest in studying the Kentucky immigration. It was there the immigrants reached the "borders of the great wilderness." From the Potomac to New River, along the valley, travel was not attended with difficulty or danger of any consequence. The wild, rough, and dangerous part of the journey commenced when New River was crossed at Inglis' Ferry, and the travelers turned squarely toward the setting sun to make their way across the mountains and streams through the "uninhabited country."

Of this interesting locality—the crossing at New River —I will make a brief mention, chiefly from information furnished me by Colonel J. Marshall McCue and Dr. John P. Hale, of West Virginia.

Colonel Abraham Wood, who lived at the Falls of the Appomattox in 1744, made a hunting, exploring, and trading expedition along the east of the Blue Ridge to where the Dan and the little river of New River nearly meet at a gap, through which he passed, calling it Wood's Gap, which name it still retains. He went down Little River to New River, almost in sight of the present Inglis' Ferry. He reached New River and called it Wood's River, and that name it bore for a long time.

Dr. Thomas Walker also, who lived at Castle Hill, Albermarle County, Va., penetrated these wilds in 1750. He went by Staunton and up the valley, crossing the Alleghany on the water shed at the present site of Blackberry, crossed New River at Horseshoe, went down the river to the mouth of Walker's Creek, and up the creek along the face of Walker's Mountain to the head waters of Clinch River. Passing down the Clinch he made his way to the gap to which he gave the name of Cumberland, also giving the same name to the range of mountains which then bore the Indian name, Ousiotto. Proceeding into the land of Kentucky he named Cumberland River, and called Kentucky River "Louisa." He gave these names in honor of the Duke of Cumberland and the Duke's wife.

About the same time the Inglis and Draper families, starting from Pattonsburg, on the James River, settled where Dr. Walker crossed the Alleghany divide, now called Blackberry. They were the first families to pitch their tents west of the Alleghanies. They called their settlement "Draper's Meadows." The land was afterward acquired by William Preston, and by him called Smithfield.

In 1755 this settlement was raided by Shawnee Indians from the Scioto Valley. Several persons were killed and others taken prisoners and carried off to Ohio. In the summer and fall of that year, 1755, Wm. Inglis and John Draper, whose wives had been made prisoners, started down into the Cherokee territory to look for them, not knowing in what direction they had been taken. The route taken by Inglis and Draper afterward became the great traveled way from Virginia to Kentucky. They did not succeed in finding the women, but Mrs. Mary Inglis was carried to the mouth of the Scioto, where the Shawnees had a town, and thence to Big Bone Lick, where she made her escape, and after incredible sufferings and wanderings, through several hundred miles of wilderness, she made her way back home. Her story is one of the most thrilling in the early annals. She was the great-grandmother of Dr. John P. Hale.

William Inglis established the ferry over New River, known as Inglis' Ferry, and provided for the immigration which afterward came, by blazing and marking a road eastward and westward of the ferry—following westward the course which he and Draper had taken. Inglis' Ferry is a few miles above the bend in New River, known as Horseshoe, where Dr. Walker first crossed. The great immigration crossed at the ferry.

The routes of travel marked out at that day are still used. The roads which now lead through the valley of Virginia, commencing at the Potomac, and passing through Martinsburg, Winchester, Staunton, Lexington, Pattonsburg, Amsterdam, Salem, Big Spring, Christianburg, Inglis' Ferry, Newbern, Mac's Meadows, Wytheville, Marion, Abingdon are the same which were laid out and traveled in the early days.

Beside the road which passed along the valley of Virginia, and the one which ran out from Richmond to the intersection at New River, there were other traveled ways or traces which led up to Cumberland Gap from the Carolinas and through the mountains of East Tennessee.

Thus it appears that all the roads from the Atlantic States converged upon two points, Fort Pitt and Cumberland Gap.

John Filson, in his history of the discovery and settlement of Kentucky, published in 1784, and which is even more rare than that of Imlay, has left an itinerary of the upper Pennsylvania road from Philadelphia to Fort Pitt, and also of the overland route to Kentucky, from Philadelphia through the valley of Virginia and Cumberland Gap, and through the mountains and interior parts of Kentucky to the Falls of the Ohio. They are of sufficient interest to be reproduced here—especially as Filson's book is extremely rare.

The table of places and distances on the road from Philadelphia to Fort Pitt is as follows:

	MILES		MILES
From Philadelphia to Lancaster, .	66	To Juniata Creek, ...	19
To Middletown, ...	26	To Bedford, ...	14
To Harris' Ferry, ...	10	To Foot of Alleghany Mountains,	15
To Carlisle, ...	17	To Stony Creek, ...	15
To Shippenburg, ...	21	To East side Laurel Hill, . .	12
To Chamberstown, ...	11	To Fort Ligonier, ...	9
To Fort Loudon, ...	13	To Pittsburgh, ...	54
To Fort Littleton, ...	18		

A total distance of 320 miles.

Filson's itinerary of the Journey from Philadelphia to the Falls of the Ohio by land is as follows:

	MILES		MILES
From Philadelphia to Lancaster,	66	To Washington C. H.,	45
To Wright's on the Susquehanna,	10	To the Block-house,	35
To Yorktown,	12	To Powell Mountain,	33
To Abbottstown,	15	To Walden's Ridge,	3
To Hunterstown,	10	To Valley Station,	4
To mountain at Black's Gap,	3	To Martin's Cabin,	25
To other side the mountain,	7	To Cumberland Mountain,	20
To Stone-house Tavern,	25	To Cumberland River,	13
To Wadkin's Ferry on Potomac,	14	To Flat Lick,	9
To Martinsburg,	13	To Stinking Creek,	2
To Winchester,	13	To Richland Creek,	7
To Newtown,	8	Down Richland Creek,	8
To Stoverstown,	10	To Raccoon Spring,	6
To Woodstock,	12	To Laurel River,	2
To Shenandoah River,	15	To Hazel Patch,	15
To North Branch Shenandoah,	29	To Rockcastle River,	10
To Staunton,	15	To English Station,	25
To North Fork James River,	37	To Col. Edwards', Crab Orchard,	3
To Botetourt C. H.,	12	To Whitley's Station,	5
To Woods on Catawba River,	21	To Logan's Station,	5
To Paterson's on Roanoke,	9	To Clark's Station,	7
To Alleghany Mountain,	8	To Crow's Station,	4
To New River,	12	To Harrod's Station,	3
To Forks of Road,	16	To Harlands',	4
To Fort Chissel,	12	To Harbisons,	10
To Stone Mill,	11	To Bardstown,	25
To Boyds,	8	To Salt Works,	25
To Head of Holstein,	5	To Falls of the Ohio,	20

A total distance of 826 miles.

The following itinerary, with "observations and occurrences," was kept by William Brown, the father of Judge Alfred M. Brown, of Elizabethtown, Ky. It is contained in a small manuscript book, which has been preserved in the family. It is especially interesting from the fact that immediately upon his arrival in Kentucky, by the journey of which he made a complete record, the battle of Blue Licks occurred. He aided in burying the slain, among whom was his own brother, James Brown.

William Brown's Route to Kentucky, in 1782.

	MILES		MILES
To Richmond, Henrico Co.,	18	To 7-mile Ford of Holstein,	6
To Widow Simpson's, Chesterford,	14	To Maj. Dysart's Mill,	12
To Powhatan Co. House,	16	To Washington Co. House,	10
To Joseph Thompson's, at the forks of the road,	8	To Head of Reedy Creek, Sullivan Co., North Carolina,	20
To Long's Ordinary, Buckingham,	9	To Block House,	13
To Hoolen's, on Willis Creek,	8	To North Fork Holstein,	2
To Mrs. Sanders, Cumberland,	3	To Moccasin Gap,	5
To Widow Thompson's, passing Hood's and Swiney's,	27	To Clinch River,	11
To Captain Hunter's,	5	To Ford of Stock Creek,	2
To Thompson's, on the Long Mo., Campbell,	5	To Little Flat Lick,	5
To Dupriest,	6	To North Fork of Clinch,	1
To New London,	10	To Powell's Mountain,	1
To Liberty Town,	16	To Wallan Ridge,	5
To Yearley's, at Goose Creek, Bedford,	12	To Valley Station,	5
To M. Loland, at the Blue Ridge Gap,	6	To Powell's River,	2
To Big Flat Lick,	10	To Glade Spring,	4
To Fort Lewis, Botetourt,	12	To Martin's Station,	19
To Hans Meadows',	20	To Big Spring,	12
To English's Ferry, New River,	12	To Cumberland Mountain Gap,	8
To Fort Chiswell,	30	To Yellow Creek,	2
To Atkins' Ordinary,	19	To Cumberland River,	13
To Mid Fork Holstein,	—	To Big Flat Lick,	9
To Cross White's, Montgomery,	3	To Little Richland Creek,	10
To Col. Arthur Campbell's,	3	To Big Richland Creek,	1
		To Robinson Creek,	10
		To Raccoon Spring,	1
		To Laurel River,	2
		To Little Laurel River,	5

	MILES		MILES
To Raccoon Creek,	8	To English Station,	8
To Hazel Patch,	4	To Crab Orchard,	3
To Rockcastle Creek,	6	To Logan's Old Fort,	11
To Rockcastle River,	7	To Doehurty's Station,	8
To Scaggs' Creek,	5	To Harrod's Station,	6
To Head of Dicks River,	15	To Harrodsburg,	6

From Hanover to Harrodsburg is 555 miles.

Observations and Occurrences: Set out from Hanover Monday, 27th May, 1782; arrived at the Block-house about the first week in July. The road from Hanover to this place is generally very good; crossing the Blue Ridge is not bad; there is not more than a small hill with some winding to go over. Neither is the Alleghany Mountain by any means difficult at this gap. There are one or two high hills about New River and Fort Chiswell. The ford of New River is rather bad; therefore we thought it advisable to cross in the ferry-boat. This is generally a good-watered road as far as the Block-house. We waited hereabouts near two weeks for company, and then set out for the wilderness with twelve men and ten guns, this being Thursday, 18th July. The road from this until you get over Wallen's Ridge generally is bad, some part very much so, particularly about Stock Creek and Stock Creek Ridge. It is a very mountainous country hereabout, but there is some fine land in the bottoms, near the watercourses, in narrow slips. It will be but a thin-settled country whenever it is settled. The fords of Holstein and Clinch are both good in dry weather, but in a rainy season you are often obliged to raft over. From them along down Powell's Valley until you get to Cumberland Gap is pretty good; this valley is formed by Cumberland Mountain on the northwest, and Powell Mountain on the southeast, and appears to bear from northeast southwestwardly, and is, I suppose, about one hundred miles in length, and from ten to twelve miles in breadth. The land generally is good, and is an exceeding well-watered country, as well as the country on Holstein River, abounding with fine springs and little brooks. For about fifty miles, as you travel along the valley, Cumberland Mountain appears to be a very high ridge of white rocks, inaccessible in most places to either man or beast, and affords a wild, romantic prospect. The way through the gap is not very difficult, but from its situation travelers may be attacked in some places, crossing the mountain, by the enemy to a very great disadvantage. From thence until you pass Rockcastle River there is very little good road; this tract of country is very mountainous, and badly watered along the trace, especially for springs. There is some good land on the water-courses, and just on this side Cumberland River appears to be a good tract, and within a few years I expect to have a settlement on it. Some parts of the road is very miry in rainy weather. The fords of Cumberland and Rockcastle are both good unless the waters be too high; after you cross Rockcastle there are a few high hills, and the rest of the way tolerable good; the land appears to be rather weak, chiefly timbered with oak, etc. The first of the Kentucky waters you touch upon is the head of Dick's River, just eight miles from English's. Here we arrived Thursday, 25th inst., which is just seven days since we started from the Block-house. Monday, 29th inst., I got to Harrodsburg, and saw brother James. The next day we parted, as he was about setting off on a journey to Cumberland.

On Monday, August 19th, Colonel John Todd, with a party of one hundred and eighty-two of our men, attacked a body of Indians, supposed to number six or seven hundred, at the Blue Lick, and was defeated, with the loss of sixty-five persons missing and slain.

Officers lost: Colonels—John Todd and Stephen Trigg; Majors—Edward Bulger and Silas Harlan; Captains—W. McBride, John Gordon, Jos. Kincaid, and Clough Overton; Lieutenants—W. Givens, and John Kennedy; Ensign—John McMurtry.

In this action brother James fell. On Saturday, 24th inst., Colonel Logan, with four hundred and seventy men, went on the battle-ground and buried the slain; found on the field, slain, forty-three men, missing, twenty-two, in all sixty-five.

I traveled but little about the country. From English's to Harrodsburg was the farthest west, and from Logan's Fort to the Blue Lick the farthest north. Thus far the land was generally good—except near and about the Lick it was very poor and badly timbered—generally badly watered, but pretty well timbered. At Richmond Ford, on the Kentucky River, the bank a little below the ford appears to be largely upward of a hundred feet perpendicular of rock.

On my return to Hanover I set off from John Craigs' Monday, 23d September, 1782; left English's Tuesday, 1 o'clock, arrived at the Block-house the Monday evening following, and kept on the same route downward chiefly that I traveled out. Nothing material occurred to me. Got to Hanover sometime about the last of October the same year.

I have also a partial itinerary of the route from Charlotte Court-House to Kentucky. It is on a leaf of a pocket memorandum book found among the papers of my grandfather, Thos. Speed; its date is 1790. It is headed: "Distances from Charlotte Court-House to Kentucky."

	MILES		MILES
From Charlotte Court-House to Campbell Court-House,	41	To Farriss's,	5
To New London,	13	To Clinch River,	12
To Colonel James Callaway's,	3	To Scott's Station,	12
To Liberty,	13	To Cox's at Powell River,	10
To Colonel Flemming's,	28	To Martin's Station,	2
To Big Lick,	2	To — (manuscript defaced).	
To Mrs. Kent's,	20	To Cumberland Mountain,	3
To English's Ferry,	20	To Cumberland River,	15
To Carter's,	13	To Flat Lick,	9
To Fort Chissel,	12	To Stinking Creek,	2
To the Stone-mill,	11	To Richland Creek,	7
To Adkins',	16	To Raccoon Spring,	14
To Russell Place,	16	To Laurel River,	2
To Greenaway's,	14	To Hazel Patch,	15
To Washington Court-House,	6	To Rockcastle,	10
To the Block-house,	35	To — (manuscript defaced).	

The same manuscript gives the places and distances from Cumberland Gap to North Carolina as follows:

	MILES		MILES
From Cumberland Gap to Clinch Mountain,	25	To Ross's Forge,	22
To Dyer's,	10	To the Furnace,	2
To Hawkins Court-House,	15	To Yancey's,	10
To Amiss's,	3	To Beckman's,	14
		To — (manuscript defaced).	

From Virginia and the Carolinas all the immigrants naturally entered Kentucky by Cumberland Gap. The remarkable fact is that those also from Maryland and Pennsylvania went by the same route to a very large extent: the cause doubtless being the delays, difficulties, and perils of the voyage down the river.

For many years this "overland" route through the great wilderness was the only practicable way of return. The canoe or flat-boat or keel-boat could make its way down the river from Redstone, Old Fort, or from Pittsburgh, but to take any kind of craft up stream was far too tedious for ordinary travel. There are some accounts of carrying freight up stream with great difficulty and delay, many months being consumed on the trip, amid constant danger from Indians, but passengers were not carried,

From no point on the Ohio was there any way of travel directly across the country eastward. The reason of this was the Indian occupation north of the Ohio, and the difficulty of crossing the mountains and streams along any other course than that which led through Cumberland Gap.

An extract from the memorandum of a trip by Captain Van Cleve, published in the American Pioneer, vol. 2, page 220, contains a military order signed by Samuel G. Hodgson, Quartermaster, dated Fort Washington (afterward Cincinnati), May 10, 1792. The order directs Van Cleve to proceed with all dispatch from that point to Philadelphia by the most direct route, which the order specifies to be by way of Lexington, the Crab Orchard, etc.

The editor of the Pioneer adds:

"The details of the journey are omitted; the most direct route from Cincinnati to Philadelphia, it will be perceived, was by way of Lexington and Crab Orchard; hence the route was by Cumberland Mountain, Powell Valley, Abingdon, Botetourt, Lexington, and Staunton, Va.; Martinsburg, and Hagerstown, Md.; York and Lancaster, Pa."

There were traces across the mountains from the valley of Virginia into northeastern Kentucky. Dr. Thomas Walker passed over one of these traces on his return in 1750. He probably went along the upper waters of the Kanawha River. Other explorers went through the same country, but no traveled way led across it.

I will now give such an account of the opening of the road through the wilderness as I have been able to prepare from the authorities at my command.

In addition to the natural barriers of mountains and wilderness, and also the danger from savages, all of which combined prevented the occupation of the great West for so many years; the extension of settlements westward was prohibited by royal authority. The King of England, by proclamation, in 1763, had forbidden surveys or patents of land beyond the head waters of the streams which ran to the Atlantic; all beyond that limit was accorded to the Indians, and it was only here and there that a trading post or a far distant military outpost was established in the limits of this forbidden country.

In 1768, however, a treaty was made at Fort Stanwix, N. Y., by which the Indians ceded to the whites the country known as Kentucky, as far south as Tennessee River. This treaty was understood to remove all the reasons which supported the King's proclamation, and to give the white men the right to go in and occupy. An old Indian who signed the treaty seemed to so understand it, for he afterward said to Daniel Boone, at Watauga, "Brother, we have given you a fine land, but I believe you will have much trouble in settling it.

This treaty stimulated exploration. A few families had made their way westward as far as the upper waters of the Holston, and made settlements on the Watauga, and at the Wolf Hills (now Abingdon) these settlements were one hundred miles east of Cumberland Gap. It was at this time that Daniel Boone left his peaceful habitation on the Yadkin, one hundred miles further eastward, to explore the country of Kentucky. He made his way as far as the borders of the bluegrass region, and returned to his family in 1771, "with the determination," he says, "to bring them as soon as possible to live in Kentucky, which I esteemed a second paradise, at the risk of my life and fortune."

In 1773 he started with his own and five other families. This was the beginning of the immigration over the wilderness road; it was the beginning, also, of those scenes of bloodshed which marked that immigration for years thereafter.

Boone's little company reached Powell's Valley, in sight

of the Cumberland Mountains. "The aspect of those cliffs," he says, "is so wild and horrid that it is impossible to behold them without terror."

I have myself looked upon this lofty range from Powell's Valley, and I can appreciate the feeling of dread and desolation it inspired in the minds of the men, women, and children of Boone's company. They might well have supposed they had reached the abode of monsters, and a place where no man could dwell. They were far beyond the reach of human aid; before them frowned that rocky wall which became more gloomy and dismal as the sun went down behind it. To add to their terrors they were attacked by Indians; six were killed, including Boone's eldest son, James. What wonder they made their way back, disheartened and discouraged! The wonder is they were ever induced to attempt another expedition.

In less than a year Boone again passed through the Gap, and made his way to the Falls of the Ohio. He returned in sixty-two days. He was then, as he narrates, "solicited by a number of North Carolina gentlemen, that were about purchasing the lands lying on the south side of the Kentucky River from the Cherokee Indians, to attend their treaty at Watauga, in March, 1775, to negotiate with them, and mention the boundaries of the purchase. This I accepted, and at the request of the same gentlemen undertook to mark out a road in the best passage from the settlement through the wilderness to Kentucky, with such assistance as I thought necessary to employ for such an important undertaking."

The road marked out by Boone at this time led up to the Gap from the Watauga settlement, and from the Gap it followed the great "Warrior's Path" about fifty miles. The "Warrior's Path" was a trace along which the Indians traveled back and forth from their towns on the Miamis and Scioto rivers on their hunting excursions, and when warring with the tribes below. It ran in an almost direct north course from Cumberland Gap across the eastern end of Kentucky to the mouth of Scioto River. Boone's road left the Warrior's Path, and bore a more westerly course to the "Hazel Patch" and to Rockcastle River, following a buffalo trace instead of the Indian path. From Rockcastle River, still following the trace, it went up Roundstone Creek, through Boone's Gap in Big Hill, and through the present county of Madison down the course of Otter Creek to its mouth at Kentucky River. About one mile below the mouth of Otter Creek Boone established his fort, and called it Boonesborough. The total distance traversed and marked out as an elligible line of travel from Watauga to Boonesborough was over two hundred miles.

The North Carolina gentlemen, for whom Boone performed this important service, were Colonel Richard Henderson and his associates. Colonel Henderson had, early in 1775, purchased the title and claim of the Cherokee Indians to a vast extent of territory lying south of Kentucky River, and he was taking steps to occupy it under the name of Transylvania.

Henderson himself followed Boone in the same season—

the spring of 1775—with a larger company. In Powell's Valley he was joined by Benjamin Logan; Logan had only a few years before moved from Augusta County, Virginia, to the headwaters of Holston, having imbibed the spirit of western adventure. He traveled with Henderson as far as Rockcastle River; then a difference sprang up between the two. Logan disapproved of Henderson's plans, and instead of continuing along the Boone trace to Kentucky River, he took the trace which bore more westwardly, and in the direction of the Crab Orchard. This was the same that Boone had traversed when he visited the Falls of the Ohio prior to 1775. When Logan found himself fairly in the level lands, he halted and established a station which was called St. Asaphs, or Logan's Fort. It was within one mile of the present town of Stanford.

The track pursued by Logan became a more important road than the one which led to Kentucky River. It especially became known as "the road leading through the great wilderness." It led directly to Danville, which was the center of the first efforts in the direction of State establishment, and the place where the early conventions were all held. Both of these branches of the "Wilderness Road" were great highways of pioneer travel. The one led to the heart of the bluegrass region, where Lexington was built, and the other was the direct way from Cumberland Gap, through Crab Orchard, Danville, Bardstown, Bullitt's Lick, to the Falls of the Ohio.

In connection with Henderson's claim just mentioned,

General George Rogers Clark made an historic trip over the Wilderness Road in the year 1775. Some of the early settlers were then beginning to come to Kentucky by the Ohio River route. They were perplexed to know to whom the lands belonged which lay south of Kentucky River. They did not know whether Henderson really owned them, as he claimed, or whether they appertained to Virginia. General Clarke, in company with Gabriel John Jones, went to Virginia to lay the matter before the legislature, which held its sittings at Williamsburg. They had a distressing journey; the season was bad; they lost one of their horses; the travel brought on "scald feet;" they dared not kindle fires from fear of Indians. Clarke says he suffered more torment than he ever experienced before or after. They hoped to find stations at Cumberland Gap and Martin's cabin, near by, occupied, but both were abandoned. This journey of Clarke's, over five hundred miles of wilderness road, was one of the first of that splendid series of courageous and heroic services he rendered in behalf of the people of Kentucky.

Henderson was not allowed to hold the immense territory he had bargained for with the Cherokees; but in consideration of his services he was allowed a tract of two hundred thousand acres on the Ohio, at the mouth of Green River. Not the least of his services was the opening of the wilderness road by the hand of Daniel Boone.

From that time immigrants began to pour into Kentucky. Boone took out his own family with five others in the fall of 1775.

The road marked out was at best but a trace. No vehicle of any sort passed over it before it was made a wagon road by action of the State legislature, in 1795. The location of the road, however, is a monument to the skill of Boone as a practical engineer and surveyor. There is a popular idea that he was merely a hunter and fearless Indian fighter; but a consideration of his life shows that he impressed the men of his time as being a man of intellectual capacity, a sound and broad judgment, and worthy to be intrusted with many important undertakings. It required a mind of far more than ordinary caliber to locate through more than two hundred miles of mountain wilderness a way of travel which, for a hundred years, has remained practically unchanged, and upon which the State has stamped its approval by the expenditure of vast sums of money appropriated for its improvement.

The legislature of Virginia very early recognized the necessity for a wagon road to Kentucky. In 1779, four years after Boone marked out the way, an act was passed to the effect that, whereas great numbers of people are settling in the country of Kentucky, and great advantages will redound from the free and easy communication with them: commissioners were appointed to explore the country on both sides of the mountains, and trace out the most convenient site for the road, and cause it to be cleared and opened, so as to give for the present passage for travelers and pack-horses, and report the practicability of making a wagon road. The same act provided for a guard of fifty men to protect the commissioners and the laborers from Indians.

But no wagon road was made until many years thereafter. The settlers came in such greatly increasing numbers that by the year 1790 the population of Kentucky was 73,-000, and in 1800 it was 220,000. A very large proportion came over the Wilderness Road, and that way, as we have already seen, was the only practicable route for all return travel; yet it was only a track for the weary, plodding traveler on foot or horseback, whether man, woman, or child.

There is a striking difference between the route selected by the pioneers and those selected in later years for railroad construction. The one is the opposite of the other in some respects. The pioneer avoided the water-courses, the civil engineer seeks them. The pioneer went directly across the various streams east and west of the Cumberland range; he crossed the Holston, Clinch, Powell, Cumberland, and Rockcastle; he climbed and descended the mountain ridges which lay between the rivers. The civil engineer, on the contrary, in locating the railroad which connects Virginia and Kentucky, threaded the rocky defiles of New and Kanawha Rivers, and entered the level lands of the State through its northeast corner. The rugged sides of a mountain watercourse afford the poorest natural footway, and necessitate frequent crossings from side to side. In constructing a railroad, however, these obstacles are removed. The side-cut and the tunnel open a pathway unknown to the pioneer.

In no way can an understanding of the difficulties of

travel through the great wilderness be obtained so well as by study of some of the early narratives.

Felix Walker, with Captain Twetty and six others, left Rutherford, North Carolina, in February, 1775 (according to Felix Walker's narrative), "to explore the country of Leow-visay, now Kentucky." They proceeded to Watauga, where the treaty was being held by Colonel Henderson with the Indians for the purchase of the country to which they were going, then called the Bloody Ground, from the wars of hunting parties of Indians. They remained at Watauga during the treaty, which lasted twenty days; they then proceeded on their journey, and at Long Island, in the Holston River, they met Daniel Boone, Squire Boone, and Richard Calloway, with others. The two parties, when united, numbered fifty persons. Colonel Boone, "who was to be our pilot and conductor through the wilderness to the promised land," took command.

On the 10th of March they left Long Island, marking their track with hatchets. They crossed Clinch and Powell's River, passed through the Gap, crossed Cumberland River, and came to Rockcastle; leaving that river, they cut their way through a country covered with dead brush, about twenty miles, thence through thick cane for thirty miles, when "we began to discover the pleasing and rapturous appearance of the plains of Kentucky."

On the 25th of March they were at a point not far from the present site of Richmond. There they were fired upon by Indians; Captain Twetty was killed, also a negro man, and Walker himself, the narrator, was wounded. He says he was carried on a litter to Kentucky River, where "we made a station, and called it Boonesboro."

Colonel Henderson himself has also left a narrative, beginning March 20, 1775. He says that, having finished his treaty with the Indians, he set out from Watauga to "Louisa." He, with his party, stopped successively at John Shelly's, John Sevier's, Calloway's, and Captain Martin's, the latter being in Powell's Valley. There the wagons were left, as they could be taken no further. They started from thence with pack-horses, which "took a scare with their packs, running away with the same, saddle and bridle." The next day they found their goods, but two horses were missing. Just before they passed through the Gap Colonel Henderson received a letter from Mr. Luttrel's camp, that five persons had been killed "on this road to the Cantuckee by the Indians." The same day he received a letter from "Dan Boone, that his company was fired on by Indians, who killed two of his men, though he kept his ground and saved his baggage." They then crossed the Gap, and "met about forty persons returning from the Cantuckee, on account of the late murder by the Indians." They "could prevail on only one to return." They reached Cumberland River, when they "met Robert Wills and his son returning." They sent word forward to Boone that they were coming. In two days they reached Laurel River; in two more days Rockcastle River. There they met James McAfee, with eighteen persons, returning from "Canetucky." They next camped at the head waters of Dick's River. On the 18th day of April, twenty-eight days after they had left Watauga, they camped "in the eye of the rich lands." The next day they camped on Otter Creek, and the day following they reached Fort Boone. They were saluted by Boone's party firing a round of twenty-five guns, and a great rejoicing was held.

It is a natural inquiry who these persons were mentioned by Henderson as returning from Kentucky? The inquiry suggests the events closely preceding the founding of Boonesboro. Explorers and surveying parties had already been making their way down the Ohio as far as the Falls. George Washington had made surveys in the northeastern parts of Kentucky. As early as 1774 Governor Dunmore had sent Daniel Boone to conduct a party of surveyors back to Virginia. He found them and led them back by way of Cumberland Gap. There was nothing strange, therefore, that in 1775 parties of men were following the trace which was the most available way of return home after an expedition to Kentucky.

Calk's Journal.

In connection with the narratives of Walker and Henderson, the journal of William Calk becomes a most interesting document. It is the journal of a trip from Prince William County, Virginia, to Boone's Fort, on Kentucky River, dating from March 13th to May 2, 1775. The original manuscript is now in possession of Thomas Calk, near

Mount Sterling, Ky., and I give, it spelling, grammar, punctuation, etc., just as it is written—not for the purpose of directing modern criticism to these defects of composition, but as part of the history of the men who passed over these primeval roads.

The Journal of William Calk, from Prince William County, Va., to Boonesboro, Ky., from March 13, 1775, to May 2, 1775, from the original now in the possession of Thomas Calk, near Mount Sterling, Ky.

1775, Mon. 13th—I set out from prince wm. to travel to caintuck on tuesday Night our company all got together at Mr. Priges on rapadon which was Abraham hanks philip Drake Eaneck Inoith Robert Whitledge and my Self thear Abrams Dogs leg got broke by Drake's Dog.

Wednesday 15th,—We started early from priges made a good Days travel and lodge this night at Mr. Cars on North fork James River.

Thursday, 16th,—We started early it rained Chief part of the day Snowed in the Eavening very hard and was very Coald we traveled all day and got to Mr. Blacks at the foot of the Blue Ridge.

Friday 17th—We started early cross the Ridge the wind Blowsz very hard and cold and lodge at James loyls.

Saturday 18th—We get this day to William Andersons at Crows ferry and there we stay till monday morning.

Monday 20th—We start early cross the ferry and lodge this night at Wm. Adamses on the head of Catauby.

Tuesday 21st—We start early and git over pepers ferry on new river and lodge at pepers this night.

Wedns 22nd—We start early and git to foart Chissel whear we git some good loaf Bread and good whiskey.

thurs 23d—we start early and travel to a good while in the Night and git to major Cammells on holston river.

fryday 24th—we start early and turn out of the wagon Road to go across the mountains to go by Danil Smiths we loose Driver Come to a turable mountain that tired us all almost to death to git over it and we lodge this night on the Lawrel fork of holston under a grait mountain and Roast a fine fat turkey for our suppers and Eat it without aney Bread.

Satrd 25th—We start early over Some more very Bad mountains one that is caled Clinch mountain and we git this night to Danil Smiths on Clinch and there we staid till thursday morning on tuesday night and wednesday morning it snowed Very hard and was very Coald and we hunted a good deal there while we staid in Rough mountains and kild three deer and one turkey Eanock Abram and I got lost tuesday night and it a snowing and Should a lain in the mountains had not I a had a pocket compas by which I got in a littel in the night and fired guns and they heard them and caim in By the Repoart.

thursd 30th—We set out again and went down to Elk gardin and there suplid our Selves With Seed Corn and irish tators then we went on a littel way I turned my hors to drive before me and he got scard ran away threw Down the Saddel Bags and broke three of our powder goards and Abrams beast Burst open a walet of corn and lost a good Deal and made a turrabel flustration amongst the Reast of the Horses Drakes mair run against a sapling and noct it down we cacht them all agin and went on and lodged at John Duncans.

fryd 31st—We suplyed our Selves at Dunkans with a 103 pounds of Bacon and went on again to Brileys mill and suployed our Selves with meal and lodged this night on Clinch By a large cainbraike and cuckt our Suppers.

April Saturday 1st—This morning there is ice at our camp half inch thick we start early and travel this Day along a verey Bad hilley way cross one creek whear the horses almost got mired some fell in and all wet thier loads we cross Clinch River and travell till late in the Night and camp on Cove creek having two men with us that wair pilates.

Sund 2d—this morning is a very hard frost we start early travel over powels mountain and camp in the head of Powels valley whear there is verey good food.

mond 3rd—We start early travel Down the valey cross powels river go some through the woods without aney track cross some Bad hills git in to hendersons Road camp on a creek in powels valey.

Tuesday 4th—Raney we Start about 10 oclock and git down to Capt. martins in the valey where we over take Col. henderson and his Company

Bound for Caintuck and there we camp this Night there they were Broiling and Eating Beef without Bread.

Wednesday 5th—Breaks away fair and we go on down the valey and camp on indian Creek we had this creek to cross maney times and very bad banks Abrams saddel turned and the load all fell in we got out this Eaavening and kill two Deer.

thursd 6th—this morning is a hard frost and we wait at Camp for Col. henderson and company to come up they come up about 12 o'clock and we join with them and camp there still this night waiting for some part of the companey that had their horses ran away with their packs.

fryday 7th—this morning is a very bad snowey morning we still continue at Camp being in number about 40 men and some neagros this Eaven-Comes a letter from Capt. Boone at caintuck of the indians doing mischief and some turns back.

Saturday 8th—We all pack up and started crost Cumberland gap about one oclock this Day   Met a good maney peopel turned Back for fear of the indians but our Company goes on Still with good courage we come to a very ugly Creek with steep Banks and have it to cross several times on this Creek we camp this night.

Sunday 9th—this morning we wait at camp for the cattel to Be drove up to kill a Beef tis late before they come and peopel makes out a little snack and agree to go on till Night we git to cumberland River and there we camp meet 2 more men turn Back.

Monday 10th—this is a lowry morning and very like for Rain and we keep at Camp this day and some goes out a hunting and I and two more goes up a very large mountain near the tops we saw the track of two indians and whear they had lain under some Rocks some of the company went over the River a bufelo hunting but found none at night Capt. hart comes up with his packs and there they hide some of thier lead to lighten thier packs that they may travel faster.

tuesday 11th—this a very loury morning and like for Rain but we all agree to start Early and we cross Cumberland River and travel Down it about 10 miles through some turrabel cainbrakes as we went down abrams mair Ran into the River with her load and swam over he followed her and got on her and made her swim back agin it is a very raney Eavening we take up Camp near Richland Creek they kill a beef Mr. Drake Bakes Bread without washing his hands we Keep Sentry this Night for fear of the indians.

Wednesday 12th—this is a Raney morning But we pack up and go on we come to Richland Creek it is high we tote our packs over on a tree and swim our horses over and there we meet another Companey going Back they tell such News Abram and Drake is afraid to go aney farther there we camp this night.

thursday 13th—this morning the weather seems to brake and Be fair Abram and Drake turn Back we go on and git to loral River we come to a creek Before wheare we are able to unload and to take our packs over on a log this day we meet about 20 more turning Back we are obliged to toat our packs over loral river and swim our horses one hors ran in with his pack and lost it in the river and they got it agin.

fryday 14th—this is a clear morning with a smart frost we go on and have a very miry Road and camp this night on a creek of loral river and are surprised at camp by a wolf.

Satterday 15th—clear with a Small frost we start early we meet some men that turns and goes With us we travel this Day through the plais caled the Bressh and cross Rockcass river and camp ther this Night and have fine food for our horses.

sunday 16th—cloudy and warm we start early and go on about 2 miles down the river and then turn up a creek that we crost about 50 times some very bad foards with a great Deal of very good land on it in the Eavening we git over to the waters of Caintuck and go a little down the creek and there we camp keep sentel the fore part of the night it Rains very har all night.

monday 17th—this is a very rany morning But breaks about a 11 oclock and we go on and camp this Night in several companeys on some of the creeks of Caintuck.

tuesday 18th—fair and cool and we go on about 10 oclock we meet 4 men from Boons camp that caim to cunduck us on we camp this night just on the Beginning of the good land near the Blue lick they kill 2 bofelos this Eavening.

wednesday 19th—smart frost this morning they kill 3 bofelos about 11 oclock we come to where the indians fired on Boons company and killed 2 men and a dog and wounded one man in the thigh we campt this night on otter creek.

thursday 20th—this morning is clear and cool. We start early and git Down to caintuck to Boons foart about 12 o'clock where we stop they come out to meet us and welcome us in with a voley of guns.

fryday 21st—warm this Day they begin laying off lots in the town and preparing for people to go to work to make corn.

Satterday 22nd—they finish laying out lots this Eavening I went a-fishing and caught 3 cats they meet in the night to draw for chose of lots but prefer it till morning.

Sunday 23rd—this morning the pecpel meets and draws for chois of lots this is a very warm day.

monday 24th—We all view our lots and some Dont like them about 12 oclock the combses come to town and Next morning they make them a bark canew and set off down the river to meet their Companey.

tuesday 25th—in the eavening we git us a plaise at the mouth of the creek and begin clearing.

Wednesday 26th—We Begin Building us a house and a plaise of Defense to Keep the indians off this day we begin to live without bread.

thursday 27th—Raney all Day But We Still keep about our house.

Satterday 29th—We git our house kivered with Bark and move our things into it at Night and Begin housekeeping Eanock Smith Robert Whitledge and myself.

May, Monday 1st—I go out to look for my mair and saw 4 bufelos the Being the first that I saw and I shot one of them but did not git him when I caim Home Eanock and Robin had found the mair and was gone out a hunting and did not come in for — Days and kild only one Deer.

tuesday 2nd—I went out in the morning and killed a turkey and come in and got some on for my breakfast and then went and sot in to clearing for Corn.

The accounts of the travel over the Wilderness Road excite admiration for the courage and hardihood of the bold men who inaugurated and guided it; they also arouse strong sympathy for the women and children who cheerfully shared the privations it entailed on them.

There is a deep pathos in the story of that great journeying, as the imagination readily pictures the companies of men, women, and children moving through the wilderness.

Consider, for instance, the number, character, and condition of the congregation of Rev. Lewis Craig's church, which moved in a body from Virginia to Kentucky. In a history of the Baptist Church in Virginia, published by Robert B. Semple, in Richmond, 1810, it is stated that "Craig's church, which was formerly called Upper Spottsylvania, is the oldest constitution between the James and Rappahannock rivers. . . . But in 1781, to the great mortification of the remaining members, Mr. Craig, with most of the church, removed to Kentucky."

Taylor, in his History of Ten Baptist Churches, states that upon his arrival in Kentucky he gave in his membership to this church, at Gilbert's Creek. "This," says he, "had been one of the traveling churches from Virginia to Kentucky; Lewis Craig, with a great number of the members of his church in Spottsylvania, had removed to Kentucky. As I have been told, they were constituted when they started, and was an organized church on the road."

Such a company journeying through the wilderness was an impressive scene. The voice of their pastor can be heard encouraging them with sermons drawn from the Exodus of the Israelites. While they enjoyed the good fortune of fair weather, sunshine, and immunity from Indian molestation, we can hear their cheerful voices in happy conversation, shouts, and songs. But when the clouds lowered, and rain, sleet, and snow were driven against them by the bleak mountain winds, we can see the distress of the women, and hear the pitiful cry of the little ones. If, to the dismal wretched-ness of rough, wild country and stormy weather, were added the horrors of an Indian attack, the picture of helpless dis-tress is complete.

Rev. Peter Cartwright, in an account of his life, says his parents came to Kentucky shortly after the Revolution, which probably means 1783. He says:

"It was an unbroken wilderness from Virginia to Kentucky at that early day. . . . There were no roads for carriages, and though the immigrants moved by thousands, they had to move on pack-horses. The fall my father moved there were a great many families who joined together for mutual safety. Besides the two hundred families thus united there were one hundred young men well armed, who agreed to guard the families through the wilderness. We rarely traveled a day, after we struck the wil-derness, but we passed some white persons murdered and scalped by the Indians."

He adds that when they were only seven miles from the Crab Orchard, which was the first white settlement they reached, seven families of their train determined to encamp for the night. The others went on to the station. That night the families which remained behind were attacked by Indians and all killed except one man.

Mrs. Julia A. Tevis, in her autobiography, says:

"At the time my grandfather, with his brothers and sisters, came to Kentucky, many families traveled together for mutual safety and protection against the Indians, whose hunting grounds extended to the border settle-ments of Virginia. On their way through the wilderness they encountered bear, buffalo, wolves, wild-cats, and sometimes herds of deer. Thus they moved cautiously onward in long line through a narrow bridle-path, so encumbered with brush and underwood as to impede their progress, and render it necessary that they should sometimes encamp for days in order to rest their weary pack-horses, and forage for themselves."

Chief Justice Robertson, in his address at Camp Madison, Franklin County, Ky., in 1843, speaking of the effect of the land law of 1779, drew this picture:

"This beneficent enactment brought to the country during the fall and winter of that year an unexampled tide of emigrants, who, exchanging all the comforts of their native society and homes for settlements for themselves and their children here, came like pilgrims to a wilderness to be made secure by their arms and habitable by the toil of their lives. Through privations incredible and perils thick, thousands of men, women, and children came in successive caravans, forming continuous streams of human beings, horses, cattle, and other domestic animals, all moving onward along a lonely and houseless path to a wild and cheerless land. Cast your eyes back on that long procession of missionaries in the cause of civilization; behold the men on foot with their trusty guns on their shoulders, driving stock and leading pack-horses; and the women, some walking with pails on their heads, others riding with children in their laps, and other children swung in baskets on horses, fastened to the tails of others going before; see them encamped at night expecting to be massacred by Indians; behold them in the month of December, in that ever memorable season of unprecedented cold called the 'hard winter,' traveling two or three miles a day, frequently in danger of being frozen or killed by the falling of horses on the icy and almost impassable trace, and subsisting on stinted allowances of stale bread and meat; but now lastly look at them at the destined fort, perhaps on the eve of merry Christmas, when met by the hearty welcome of friends who had come before, and cheered by fresh buffalo meat and parched corn, they rejoice at their deliverance, and resolve to be contented with their lot."

He adds:

"This is no vision of the imagination, it is but an imperfect description of the pilgrimage of my own father and mother, and of many others who settled in Kentucky in December, 1779."

An old pioneer author, Doddridge, strains the language to convey an idea of the desolation and solitude of the wilderness.   He says:

"One prominent feature of the wilderness is its solitude.   Those who plunged into the bosom of this forest left behind them not only the busy hum of men, but of domesticated animal life generally.   The parting rays of the setting sun did not receive the requiem of the feathered songsters of the grove, nor was the blushing aurora ushered in by the shrill clarion of the domestic fowl.   The solitude of the night was interrupted only by the howl of the wolf, and by the melancholy moan of the ill-boding owl, or the shriek of the frightful panther.   Even the faithful dog, the only steadfast companion of man among the brute creation, partook of the silence of the desert; the discipline of his master forbade him to bark or move but in obedience to his command, and his native sagacity soon taught him the propriety of obedience to this severe government."

McMaster, in his fascinating history of the People of the United States, speaks of the rapidity and extent of this emigration as unparalleled.   The authorities show that in 1783 the population of Kentucky was 12,000, and by the spring of 1784 it was 20,000.   One authority states that during that year, 1784, thirty thousand immigrants came from Virginia and North Carolina.   All these hosts of emigrants, men, women, and children, have passed away, but many persons are now living who, in their younger days, heard their fathers and mothers tell how they came out on foot to Kentucky in the great immigration over the Wilderness Road, or down the Ohio River in flat-boats.

The greater portion came through the wilderness.   It will be observed that the two routes of travel, the one through

the wilderness, and the other by the river, naturally came together at the Falls of the Ohio. From Cumberland Gap
the road is almost a straight course through Crab Orchard,
Danville, and Bardstown, to the Falls, following the natural
topography of the country. Muldrow's Hill is a continuous
range circling from the vicinity of Crab Orchard to the Ohio
River below the mouth of Salt River, a distance of more
than one hundred and twenty-five miles. Inside this circle,
extending twenty or twenty-five miles from the base of the
range, the land is generally level. In this level, following
the circle of Muldrow's Hill, the railroad now runs through
Lebanon and Crab Orchard. So the early settlers coming
into the State, having passed the mountains, reached the
level lands about Crab Orchard, or turned toward the bluegrass region along Boone's road to the Kentucky River and
beyond. Of those who passed beyond Crab Orchard, some
stopped at the nearer stations about Danville, while others
moved on to Bardstown and to the Salt Licks at Shepherds-
ville. In this country the tide from the mountains met the
tide from the river, and the emigrants from Virginia and
the Carolinas commingled with those from Maryland and
Pennsylvania.

It is noticeable also that the course of travel which led
directly up from the Cumberland Gap to the Ohio Falls,
continued in almost a direct line still westward to the
old French Fort St. Vincent, now Vincennes, and still onward to the Mississippi at St. Louis.

The great immigration from 1775 to 1795, a period of twenty years, was a movement on foot. Many of the accounts of the foot-travel of that day, if not authenticated beyond question, would read like fables of antiquity. Boone, in going from the settlement on Clinch River to the Ohio Falls in 1774, walked eight hundred miles in sixty-two days. He made many trips back and forth over the Wilderness Road. Taken prisoner at one time by the Indians he escaped at Chillicothe, and fled back to Boonesboro, a distance of more than one hundred and fifty miles, in four days. His entire life was one of constant activity; yet he never comes before the mind as a horseman, it is only as a hunter and Indian fighter on foot that he is ever thought of. An equestrian statue to Daniel Boone would be as unfitting as to associate him with a locomotive.

There is an incident in the life of Benjamin Logan which most powerfully illustrates the foot-travel of that day. Logan's Fort, on the Wilderness Road, was besieged, in May, 1777, by a force of one hundred Indians. The men fought them off while the women molded bullets; but powder and lead began to fail. There was no supply short of the older settlements on the Holston River, two hundred miles distant. In this dire extremity Logan determined to undertake the incredible task of obtaining ammunition from that distant quarter. He encouraged his men to hold the fort, crept cautiously through the Indian lines at night, and flew, we may almost say, over the wild rough mountains to the Holston settlements, procured the powder and lead, retraced his steps, and was in the fort in ten days from the time of his departure. His return gave fresh courage to the garrison, and the fort was successfully defended until a relieving force under Colonel Bowman came up, and the Indians retired.

Captain Estill, who lost his life in the bloody battle of 1782 known as Estill's defeat, rendered great services to the emigrants as they came in over the Wilderness Road. With a company of men he would meet them and escort them into the settlements. It is a tradition that his custom was to kill animals on the road, and, leaving them, he would pass on and notify incoming trains where they might find a supply of meat. His death was a great calamity, occurring as it did when the settlers most needed the protection his bravery and experience could afford.

If the light of authentic history were not so clear, revealing the real persons and the real life of the pioneers—if they were seen through the veil of misty tradition—men like Boone, Logan, Clarke, and Estill might easily become magnified to the proportions of the fabled heroes of antiquity.

The exploits of Boone stimulated the genius of Byron, but his lines are not worthy of the poet or the subject. They are not so descriptive as those of a less famous poet, Daniel Bryan, of Rockingham County, Virginia, whose "Mountain Muse," published in 1813, recounts in heroic verse "The Adventures of Daniel Boone." The volume is extremely rare. The following extract tells how Boone opened the Wilderness Road:

On Clinch till the succeeding summer shone,
Boone with his worthy family remained;
He then, successively, in dangerous toils
Of high import engaged—at Dunmore's call
He lent his guidance to conduct a band
Of brave surveyors of the Western soil
From the Ohio Falls back to their homes,
By routes through the dark wilderness to them
Before unknown.   This perilous task performed
With most surprising safety, skill, and speed,
He then of three militia garrisons,
At Dunmore's requisition, took command,
And with his wonted energy and fire,
Attempered by serene deliberate art,
Through the campaign against the Shawnese tribes,
A service marked with high success sustained.
Victorious from the northern scenes of blood,
Subservient to his countrymen's request,
We see our hero cross the desert stage
And on its southern border rise to view,
Performing there a new but arduous part,
Evincing talents versatile as strong;
And, skilled as well in council as in war,
He meets the Sachems of the Cherokees
At wild Watauga, and a pact concludes,
By virtue of his delegated powers,
For purchasing a part of their waste lands.
This embassy accomplished, he collects
A band of hardy woodsmen, strong and brave,
And from the verge of the rough wilderness,
Where Holston's mountain-compassed current rolls
To wild Kentucky's cedar-shadowed waves,
A road through the unwounded forest cleaves.

A better tribute than either Byron's or Bryan's is that of
Theodore O'Hara, in his Dirge for the old Pioneer. The following stanza commemorates Boone's labors in opening the

Wilderness Road which led civilization from the Atlantic strand into the boundless plains of the West:

> A dirge for the brave old pioneer!
>   Columbus of the land!
> Who guided freedom's proud career
>   Beyond the conquered strand,
> And gave her pilgrim sons a home
>   No monarch's step profanes,
> Free as the chainless winds that roam
>   Upon its boundless plains.

Improvements of the Wilderness Road.

In the year 1780 the County of Kentucky was divided into three counties by act of the Virginia Legislature. They were Jefferson, Fayette, and Lincoln. The points selected to serve as the county-seats respectively, were Louisville, which was the terminus of the Ohio River route, Lexington, toward which Boone's branch of the Wilderness Road directly led, and Harrodsburg, which was reached by the Crab Orchard branch; but there was no improvemet in the roads for twelve years. An immense population made its toilsome way over the natural trace. It was not until 1792 that an effort was made to provide a better way of travel for the still inpouring tide of immigrants. In that year, according to an account book recently found among the Harry Innis Papers, by Colonel John Mason Brown, a member of this society, a scheme was projected for the clearing and improvement of the Wilderness Road, under the direction of

Colonel John Logan and James Knox. It was a private enterprise altogether; the subscribers to it are set down in the book as follows:

Isaac Shelby, ...	£3 os	Matthew Walton, . . . £1 16s
Robert Breckinridge, . .	2 8	John Jouett, ... 1 10
George Nicholas, . . .	2 8	Robert Abel, ... 12
Henry Pawling, ...	1 10	John Wilson, ... 12
John Brown, ...	2 8	Richard Taylor, ... 1 10
James Brown, . . .	1 16	Arthur Fox, ... 1 0
Alexander S. Bullitt, . .	2 8	John Caldwell, ... 12
Wm. McDowell, ...	1 10	George Thompson, . . . 1 4
Edward S. Thomas, . .	1 10	Baker Ewing, ...
Joseph Crockett, . .	1 18	Abe Buford, ... 1 8
Wm. King, ...	10	Willis Green, ... 1 10
Wm. Montgomery, jr., . .	1 10	Wm. Montgomery, sr., . . 1 10
John Hawkins, ...	1 10	Morgan Forbes, ... 18
Samuel Woods, ...	1 4	Daniel Hudgins, . . . 6
Hubbard Taylor, . . .	2 8	Samuel Grundy, ... 1 10
Thomas Todd, ...	1 10	James Hays, ... 1 10
Wm. Steele, ...	1 10	James Edwards, ... 9
James Trotter, ...	1 18	Wm. Campbell, ... 12
Joseph Gray, ...	2 2	David Stevenson, . . . 9
Joshua Hobbs, ...	1 4	Hugh Logan, ... 6
Robert Todd, ...	1 10	Peter Troutman, ... 12
Jesse Cravens, ...	1 10	Thomas Montgomery, . . 6
David Knox, ...	1 12	John Vauhn, ... 6
Thomas Lewis, ...	1 10	Elijah Cravens, ... 6
Samuel Taylor, ...	1 4	Richard Chapman, . . . 6
John McKinney, . . .	1 18	James Sutton, ... 3
Nicholas Lewis, ...	1 4	Joseph Lewis, ... 6
Jacob Froman, ...	3 0	Wm. Baker, ... 6
Richard Young, ...	1 4	Richard Jackman, . . . 6
James Davies, ...	1 10	Jonathan Forbes, . . . 12
Robert Patterson, . . .	1 10	Isaac Hite, ... 12
Robert Mosby, ...	1 10	John Blane, ... 12
John Watkins, ...	1 4	Abraham Hite, ... 12

John Caldwell,	£1 4s	Samuel McDowell,	£1 4s
Peyton Short,	1 10	James Parberry,	3 0
George M. Bedinger,	18	Joseph Reed,	2 0
Alex. D. Orr,	1 10	Wm. Perrett,	5
Philip Caldwell,	1 4	John Robinson,	2 0
Cornelius Beatty,	1 16	John Wilkins,	4
Nathaniel Hart,	1 4	Wm. Whilley,	Bacon acct.
John Grant,	1 10	Henry Clark,	6
Andrew Holmes,	1 16	Hardy Rawles,	2 0
Alex. Parker,	1 16	James Young,	12
Robert Barr,	2 8	John Warren,	6
James Parker,	1 16	Peter Sidebottom,	6
Thomas Kennedy,	3 0	John Willey,	6
Wm. Live,	1 18	Moses Collier,	12
George Teagarden,	18	Abraham Himberlin,	1 0
George Muter,	1 10	Alex. Blane,	12
James Hughes,	1 10	John Jones,	18
Buckner Thruston,	1 10	Levi Todd,	1 0
John Moylan,	1 10	Thomas Ball,	12

Besides these, it appears from a note in the memorandum book there were other subscribers. Among the Innis papers I have found the following paper:

"Colonel John Logan and Colonel James Knox, having consented to act as commissioners to direct and supervise the making and opening a road from the Crab Orchard to Powell's Valley, provided funds to defray the necessary expenses shall be procured, we, the subscribers, do therefore severally engage to pay the sum annexed to our names to the Hon. Harry Innis and Colonel Levi Todd, or to their order, in trust, to be by them applied to the payment of the reasonable expenses which the said commissioners may incur in carrying the above design into effect, also to the payment of such compensation to the said commissioners for their services as the said Innis and Todd may deem adequate.

June 20, 1792.

Thos. Barber,	$10	David Rice,	$1
Wm. Crow,	5	John Rochester,	10

Green Dorsey, ...	$18	John Rogers, ...	$1
John Cochran, ...	4	Samuel G. Keen, ...	5
David Gillis, ...	10	Patrick Curran, ...	1
Wm. Petty, ...	1	John Reedyun, ...	1
John Warren, ...	10	Daniel Barber, ...	1
Wm. Kenton, ...	1	Philip Yeiser, ...	3
Philip Bush, jr., ...	10		

The money subscribed was disbursed by Harry Innis. Men were employed as "road cutters," as "surveyors," to "carry provisions," to "grind corn," and "collect bacon." The pay was two shillings sixpence per day, and the work extended over twenty-two days in the summer of 1792.

The legislature of Kentucky very promptly, upon the establishment of the State, gave attention to this great highway, and for many years thereafter it was a beaten thoroughfare, by which traders with droves of stock found their way to the Carolinas.

The first legislative act touching the subject was in 1793. Its object was to make provision for guarding the road. It provided that, whereas it has been judged expedient to enlist men to garrison the block-houses on the Wilderness Road, the men so enlisted were allowed the additional pay which is allowed to the State militia when called into the service of the United States.

In 1794 an act was passed appointing commissioners to raise a fund for clearing a road from Madison Court-house to Hazel Patch, where it would intersect the road leading from the Crab Orchard to Powell's Valley. The road thus provided for was along Boone's trace, made by him from the vicinity of Rockcastle River to Boonesboro.

In 1795 the legislature passed an act entitled, "An Act opening a Wagon Road to Cumberland Gap." The act recites that, "Whereas it is essential to the true interests of this commonwealth that a good road should be made to Virginia, . . . and whereas the General Assembly is desirous that no impediment may stand in the most speedy and beneficial execution" of the work, and is *willing that the largest sum that the present state of the public funds will admit of should be consigned for that purpose,*" an appropriation of two thousand pounds was made.

By the terms of the act the road was to commence in the neighborhood of the Crab Orchard, and from thence through the Hazel Patch, and "terminate on the top of Cumberland Mountain, in the Gap through which the present road passes." The road to be perfectly commodious for carriages and wagons carrying as much as one ton weight.

In 1797 the legislature appropriated five hundred pounds for the repair of the road and erection of a toll-gate, or "turnpike," as it is called in the act. After that date many appropriations were made for the improvement of the road. It came to be called the Wilderness Turnpike, but it never became such a road as the term "turnpike" usually signifies. It was only a natural mountain road, worked and repaired, and furnished with bridges and ferries.

The Ohio River Route.

It would naturally seem that the way to Kentucky by
the Ohio River would have been preferred to the Wilderness Road by the early immigrants. A broad, deep stream,
with a gentle current, and no obstruction from Pittsburgh
to Louisville, would strike the mind as a provision of nature,
by which population might be carried westward after passing
the mountains. But the experiences of those who made the
voyage were so severe, and the accounts which went back of
delays, hardships, and dangers were so terrifying, it excites
no wonder that the toilsome journey by way of Cumberland
Gap was selected, even by those who came from the Northern
States.

Though Pittsburgh had been a military post since 1754,
it could afford but little aid to families bound for Kentucky
in the earlier stages of the emigration. In 1775 it really
had no more inhabitants than Boone and Henderson had
gathered that same year at Boonesboro. It was ten years
afterward, when its population had reached a thousand, that
it began to be, as McMaster says, "the centering point of
emigrants to the West," from whence "travelers were carried
in keel-boats and Kentucky flat-boats and Indian pirogues
down the waters of the Ohio." The difficulty of procuring
such transportation must be taken into account. It was a
tedious process to prepare the lumber and construct boats
at that starting point in the wilderness, for Pittsburgh itself

was in the depths of the wilderness. It required courage of the highest order to put out from that post for a river voyage of weeks, and no friendly shelter or harbor at which to stop on the way. It was known that the banks were infested with Indians, and to be attacked on the water was more dreadful than upon land. The boats were rude and small; they were crowded with human beings, and their baggage and stock. It was task enough to make the voyage unmolested, and a terrible fate to encounter savages on the way. A more pitiable plight is not conceivable than a cargo of emigrants on a rude, drifting craft, fifteen feet wide by forty or fifty feet in length, helpless on the bosom of the Ohio, receiving a murderous fire from the bank.

Imlay, writing in 1792, says, at Redstone, Old Fort, or Pittsburgh, emigrants could either buy a boat at about five shillings per ton, or freight their goods to Kentucky at one shilling per hundred weight; but this was toward the close of Indian molestation. Even then there was no regular business of this sort, and emigrants must put up with delays and unsatisfactory accommodations.

To illustrate the character of the travel to Kentucky by way of the river, I will quote a passage from "Taylor's History of Ten Baptist Churches," an old and rare book. Taylor came out from Virginia in 1783. He says it was then regarded a gloomy thing to move to Kentucky. After alluding to the contemplated horrors that lay in the way, he says:

"We took water at Redstone, and from want of a better opening, I paid for a passage in a lonely, ill-fixed boat of strangers. The river being low, this lonesome boat was about seven weeks before she landed at Beargrass. Not a soul was then settled on the Ohio between Wheeling and Louisville, a space of five hundred or six hundred miles, and not one hour, day or night, in safety; though it was now winter, not a soul in all Beargrass settlement was in safety but by being in a fort. I then meditated traveling about eighty miles to Craig's Station, on Gilbert's Creek, in Lincoln County. We set out in a few days; nearly all I owned was then at stake. I had three horses, two of them were packed, the other my wife rode, with as much lumber beside as the beast could bear. I had four black people, one man, and three smaller ones. The pack horses were led, one by myself, the other by my man. The trace, what there was being so narrow and bad, we had no chance but to wade through all the mud, rivers, and creeks we came to. Salt River, with a number of its large branches, we had to deal with often ; those waters being flush, we often must wade to our middle. . . . Those struggles often made us forget the dangers we were in from Indians. . . . After six days painful travel of this kind, we arrived at Craig's Station a little before Christmas, and about three months after our start from Virginia."

The experience of Captain William Hubbell illustrates the dangers of the river route, even as late as 1791.

He procured a flat-boat on the Monongahela; nine men, three women, and eight children went on board. As they floated down the Ohio they discovered signs of Indians, and kept watch night and day. One morning about daylight a voice from the shore was heard begging to be taken on board; Captain Hubbell refused to land. The Indians, seeing their decoy was unsuccessful, attacked the flat-boat; twenty-five or thirty approached in canoes. Firing commenced on both sides. The lock of Captain Hubbell's rifle was shot off by a bullet from an Indian gun, but he coolly seized a fire-brand and fired his piece with fatal effect. His right arm was disabled, but he continued the fight, using pistols and hurling billets of wood. The Indians were driven off; but of the nine men only two remained unhurt, and three were killed. After the fight one of the children—a little boy—asked to have a bullet taken out of his head. On examination it was found that a bullet was indeed lodged in his scalp. "That ain't all," said he, showing a wound in his arm which had broken a bone. He had made no outcry, because the children had been ordered to keep quiet. The horses were all killed but one. In a space five feet square, on the side of the cabin, one hundred and twenty two bullet-holes were counted.

Other illustrations may be found in Collins' History of Kentucky, and need not be repeated here. I may add that by the indefatigable labors of R. H. Collins, LL.D., his two-volume edition of the well known work, Collins' Kentucky, has been filled with incidents of pioneer adventure, showing the dangers and hardships attending the settlement of the State.

Brown's Itinerary.

Mention has already been made of a road which led out from Richmond, following the track of Braddock's old road to Redstone, Old Fort, from which point the travel to Kentucky was by water.

The following is a very interesting itinerary of that journey, with "observations and occurrences," by William Brown.

It is copied from his same memorandum book already described. It very aptly shows the tediousness of the river route, and suggests the perils incident to it, when Indians lurked along the Ohio, especially on the "Indian side," at every point where the current might draw the drifting boat near to their murderous clutches. Not the least important information supplied by this old journal is the noting of the islands in the river from Pittsburgh to Maysville. From these data the scientist is helped to chronicle the insular changes ever occurring in the washing away of one island and the forming of another along the course of this river. Another suggestive fact recorded in this journal is the few human habitations along the river banks as late as 1790. And finally, the river pilot of to-day may compare the courses of the channel in the last century, as given in this journal, with those of the present, and philosophize upon the ever-changing currents of the Beautiful River.

William Brown's route to Kentucky, in 1790, from Hanover:

	MILES		MILES
To Hanover Co.-House,	16	To Pendleton's Ford, on Rappahannock,	10
To Edmund Taylor's,	16		
To Parson Todd's, Louisa,	20	To Douglass's Tavern, or Wickliffe's House,	13
To Widow Nelson's,	20		
To Brock's Bridge, Orange Co.,	9	To Chester's Gap, Blue Ridge,	8
To Garnet's Mill,	5	To Lehu Town,	3
To Bost. Ord'y, near Hinds' House,	7	To Ford of Shenandore River, Frederick,	2
To Raccoon Ford, on Rapidan or Porters,	6	To Stevensburg,	10
To Culpepper Co.-House,	10	To Brown's Mill,	2

	MILES		MILES
To Winchester,	6	To Big Shades of Death,	2
To Gasper Rinker's,	11	To Mountain Tav., or White	
To Widow Lewis's, Hampshire,	11	Oak Springs,	2
To Crock's Tav.,	9	To Simpson's Tav., Fayette Co.,	
To Reynold's, on the So. Branch		Pennsylvania,	6
Potowmack,	13	To Big Crossing of Yoh,	9
To Frankford Town,	8	To Carrol's Tavern,	12
To Holdeman's Mills,	4	To Laurel Hill,	6
To North Branch, Potowmack,	3	To Beason Town,	6
To Gwyn's Tav., at the Fork		To Redstone, Old Fort,	12
of Braddock's old road, Alle-		To Washington Town, Washing-	
ghany Co., Maryland,	3	ton Co., Penn.,	23
To Clark's Store,	6	To Wheeling, Old Fort, Ohio	
To Little shades of Death,	12	Co., Vir.,	35
To Tumblestone Tav., or the			
Little Meadows,	3	Total, 359 miles.	

I embarked at Redstone, Old Fort, and thence to the mo. of Yoh, 70 miles, to Fort Pitt, 20 miles.

1st Island. Just below the Mo of Alleghany Riv leave it to the left hand keep close under the Mo of Allegany as you get into the Ohio. There is a shoal about the middle of the river, here sun set Oct. 2d.

2d. Two small I, about 20 miles below Keep them to the left hand.

3rd I, about 10 miles below flat and gravelly at first appearance, rises high at the lower end—leave this to the right hand, here day broke Oct 3d. There is a small passage on The right side and here we saw an Indian.

4th I, This stands about 3 miles above the one I mention as the 3d leave this to the left hand and run close under the Indian shore.

5th Three or four small I, close together, leave them to the left hand.

6th I, hard by a small flat gravelly one keep the last at the lower end close to your left hand and leave this to the right. There appears two channels when you first get sight of this I, but the right hand one is very shoal course of River here bears N. N. W. Since the morning we passed big Domingo cr. on the In. side.

7th I, leave to the right hand.

8th I, a sand bank, a few miles below leave to the left hand, Buffalo cr. on the Virginia side below Fort Pitt, night came on and lay here till morning Oct 4th There is a little town at this place.

9th I, 3 Is, together channel on both sides The Virginia channel the most direct.

10th I, leave to the right hand.

11th I, channel good on both sides, the left hand goes by Wheeling below Buffalo.

12th 2 Is, a few miles apart leave both to the right here night came on.

13th I, at the Mo of Grave cr. on the Vir side, leave it to the left hand.

14th I, leave it to the left hand. Day break Oct 5th.

15th 2 Is, leave them to the left hand.

16th 4 Is, near together leave them to the left hand. About here Log cr. makes in from the Indian side, Keep pretty close to the In. side.

17th I, leave it to the left hand.

18th I, hard by; appears to have been two good channels as you first get sight of it; leave it to the left hand. The prospect is rather hilly here.

Distance from Redstone to Wheeling 150 miles.

19th I, channel on both sides, right hand best.

20th 2 Is, with three channels all in view keep the middle one, here you have a beautiful prospect course of river bearing S. W.

21st I, stands at the lower end of this channel, channel on each side, left hand is most direct. You are now drawing near Muskingham settlement, here night came on.

22d I, about 5 or 6 miles below the last is called Muskingham I, and here about the settlement, which is below Wheeling 100 miles. The right hand channel of this I is best.

23d I, a few miles below leave it far to the left hand and keep close under the In. shore. Day breaks Oct 6th.

24th I, leave it to the left hand hereabouts is Bellpre settlement on the In. side below Muskingham 16 miles. Little Sandy River makes in from the Vir. side hereabouts.

25th 3 small Is, leave them to the right hand.

26th I, leave it to the right hand.

27th I, hard by, right hand channel is best. Distance from Redstone to Bellpre 266 miles. Passing along you go by Bellville settlement on the Vir. side, and some houses on the In. side.

28th I, a little below Bellville leave it to the left hand, a little below the end of this I, there is a shoal in the Riv. you must steer pretty well over to the In. shore, here we got a ground and here night came on.

29th 3 or 4 Is more, leave them to the left hand. Day breaks Oct 7th.

30th I, a long one leave it to the left hand.

31st, 2 Is, leave them to the left hand, good depth of water now down to the Mo of big Canaway which is below Bellpre 74 miles. here is point Pleasant, a beautiful spot.

32d I, about 2 miles below leave it to the right hand, a little below this I is the French settlement on the the In. Shore. This day we passed by several crs. on both sides the River.

33d I, 12 miles below the point, leave it to the right hand, here night came on. We passed big Sandy River on the Vir. side. Day breaks Oct 8th. We passed big Guyandot cr. about 42 miles below the point on the Vir. side.

Distance from Redstone to P. Pleasant 340 miles at Guyandot the prospect is a little mountainous, River bearing S. W., night came on. We pass little Sciota on the In side. Day breaks Oct 9th. We are just at the Mo of Big Sciota on the In side below the Point 100 miles. Here the view is a little hilly particular on the Vir. side, and lower down on the In side are some hills. Now good depth of water down to an I, the 34th called the 10 mile I, which leave to the left hand.

35th I, 6 miles below are the 3 Is which leave to the right hand. You are now just 12 miles above Limestone. About 5 or 6 miles above Limestone there are two or three high hills on the Virg. side. There is a settlement making on the In. side opposite the 3 Is. Just before you approach Limestone there appears some few hills on the In. side. We arrived at Limestone about 3 o'clock Sunday morn, the 10th Oct just 50 miles below big Sciota.

From Redstone to Limestone is 490 miles. Set out from Limestone for Mount Gilead on Sunday morning Oct 10, 1790. Thence

	MILES		MILES
To Washington T, Washington Co.,	4	To Harrodsburg, Lincoln Co.,	11
		To Wilson Station,	27
To Mays Lick,	4	To Beech fork, Nelson Co., of	
To Blue Lick,	12	Salt Riv.,	13
To Bourbon T, Bourbon Co.,	20	To Bardstown,	7
To Lexington T, Fayette Co.,	20	To Beech fork again,	1
To Curds Ferry across Ken-tucky Riv. at Mo. of Dicks Riv.,	22	To Rolling fork of Salt Riv.,	20
		To Mount Gilead, Nolin Creek,	10

From Limestone to Mount Gilead is 171 miles.

Observations and Occurrences : Set out from Hanover Friday 6th August 1790 arrived at Redstone Old Fort about the 25th Inst. The road is pretty good until you get to the Widow Nelsons, then it begins to be hilly and continues generally so till you get to the Blue Ridge—pretty well watered. Racoon ford on Rapidan is rather bad. The little mountains are frequently in view After you pass Widow Nelsons. Pendletons ford on Rappahanock is pretty good. In going over Chester gap you ride about 5 miles among the mountains before you get clear, a good many fine springs in the Mo. between the Blue Ridge and the Allegany Mo. appears to be a fine country, altho the land is pretty much broken. At Shenandore ford there is two branches of the river to cross and it is bad fording. But there is a ferry a little below the ford. There is a very cool stream of water about 14 miles below Winchester. This is a well watered country but springs are rather scarce on the road, at Winchester there are several fine springs. The South branch of Potowmack has a good ford, also the North branch. Soon after you pass Gwyns Tavern in Maryland you enter upon the Allegany Mo. and then you have a great deal of bad road, many ridges of Mo—the Winding Ridge—Savage, Negro, etc. and Laurel hill which is the last, but before you get to the Mount, there is some stony bad road between the Widow Lewis' and the Mo. after you pass clark's store in the Mo. you get into a valley of very pretty oak land. In many places while you are in the Mo. there is very good road between the ridges. Just before you get to the Little Shades of Death there is a tract of the tallest pines I ever saw. The shades of Death are dreary looking valleys, growing up with tall cypress and other trees and has a dark gloomy appearance. Tumblestons, or the Little Meadows is a fine plantation with beautiful meadow ground. Crossing of Yoh, is a pretty good ford. There is some very bad road about here. It is said Gen Braddock was buried about 8 miles forward from this, near a little brook that crosses the road. Laurel hill is the highest ridge of the Mo. When you get to the top of it to look forward toward Redstone there is a beautiful prospect of the country below the Mo. You see at one view a number of plantations and Beason Town which is six miles off.

The country from this to Redstone is very broken tho but few of the hills so steep but they are tendable.

It is a fine grass country all along The Monongahail River, and excellent for small grain, and may be called a well watered country, tho many of their springs of water have a taste of slate or coal.

The country from Redstone to Wheeling is generally very broken well timbered with oak. The bottoms are generally fine land. It is watered much as the country about Redstone is.

I set out from Redstone down the River Monongahail on Thursday 30th Septr. The course of the River bears generally about W, until it joins the Allegany Riv. All along down are very pretty bottoms which afford excellent meadow ground and some fine plantations. A few hills, They increase in height as you draw near Fort Pitt. Yohogany River empties in this on the So side. At Redstone the River is 100 or 150 yards wide and so down until you get about Ft. Pitt It is then 2 or 3 hundred yards over.

Allegany River makes in and joins this from the Eastward, and appears to be about the same size. Right in the fork stands Ft. Pitt.

The Ohio Riv. bears from here about a N. W. course and is about ¼ of a mile wide. The point of land is high above the water and to look back upon this place as you get into the Ohio, you have a beautiful view, and were there elegant buildings, they would have much the appearance of grandeur, from the loftiness of its situation. The country from this down to Buffaloe is generally mountainous, tho none remarkably high. There are many bottoms of fertile land between the hills.

A few miles before you get to Buffaloe the river bottoms begin to appear very fertile, and continue so on down to Limestone with some few hills and ridges, you will see now and then as you pass along.

The Ohio is a beautiful river, and as you sail along you have some delightful views—The verdure of the trees—shady level banks, smooth water and great distance you can see before you in some of the reaches of the river. Ten or 12 miles above Muskingham there stands 2 Is in the river with three channels all in full view at the same time, and a very straight long reach of the river.

Here the sun was just about setting as we went down. The Is were covered with spreading green trees, and the banks of the river. It appeared to be the most enchanting view I ever beheld.

Point Pleasant is a beautiful spot. It stands about 30 feet above the water and is a perfect level. One day or other I think there will a large city be built here.

A few miles off from the Point the country is mountainous. The Canaway River falls into the Ohio from a So. course and appears to be about 400 yards wide at the Mo.

The Ohio appears to be about ¼ mile wide at this place, and also after the junction of the Canaway it appears to be the same width and is generally the case more & less from Ft. Pitt down to Limestone.

Generally near the In shore from Muskingham down there is the greatest depth of water.

Some of the Is in the river appear to be very fertile. There is a very fine I at the Mo of Wheeling belonging to Col. Zane and has a good plantation on it, and in many there may be fine plantations made. Some of the Is I mention in my list lie low and whenever the river is above a common height will be covered with water, and in that case my direction will be imperfect respecting what side to go of the Is. However in the daytime the current of water and your eye must direct you in a great measure, and in the night if it be dark you must let the current carry you, but keep a good look out to avoid running upon the trees that are stuck about in the river and the rocks of which there is not many—but a number of old trees.

To avoid running upon these if it be dark you must listen very attentively to hear the riffling of the water, and when you draw near if you find the boat getting on it, you must steer off. In a general way endeavour to keep your boat in the middle of the river with her head right down stream, and the watchman standing right in the head.

Avoid rowing at night unless necessity requires—the noise of the oars will prevent you from hearing the riffling of the water occasioned by the rocks and old trees.

In a general way the Ohio runs in a S. W. direction down to Limestone. The bank here is about 30 feet high. The road from this to Washington is bad and hilly. From thence to Kentucky river no very bad hills but a number of creeks and in wet weather is a very miry road.

You cross three branches of the Licking and the forks of Elk horn.

The country this far appears to be generally poorly timbered and badly watered, tho exceedingly rich, except about the Blue Lick the land is poor and stoney and also it is poor as you draw near Kentucky river.

A little below Curds ferry across Kentuck at the Mo of Dicks riv. the bank of the So. side appears to be largely upwards of 300 feet and some places perpendicular of rock and has a very wild appearance.

From this to Harrodsburg the road is pretty good. The land generally is but middling and not very well timbered. Thence to Wilsons—crossing several branches of Salt riv. The land is generally good and some exceeding fine and well timbered and pretty well watered, the road is pretty good. From thence to the waters of Nolin the land is generally pretty good Bardstown stands in a bend of the beech fork and is a tolerable pretty place—lies level.

The beech fork is about 50 yards wide. The rolling fork not quite so broad. Some distance before you get to Nolin you will find poor land on the road as also the Barrens begin.

These plains are generally good land for wheat and turn out pretty well in corn.

They afford excellent range for stock.

The timbered land in this part of the country is chiefly on the water courses.

It is pretty well watered and is much the pleasantest of any part of Kentucky I ever was in.

I arrived at Mount Gilead Oct 17 on Sunday 1790.

Set out from Mount Gilead Tuesday 2d Nov. 90, and took the road that goes by Pottengers, Hadens Lewis, Thomas, Sanduskys. On the trace there is a good deal of good land and well timbered some excellent oak timbered land.

Route to Tennessee and Western Kentucky.

Another route by which certain portions of Kentucky were settled must be noticed. Prior to 1783 immigrants who desired to settle in the country of *Cumberland*, as the middle portion of Tennessee was then called, came first into Kentucky by the Wilderness Road, through Cumberland Gap, and proceeded as far as the Rockcastle hills. From thence they turned southward and followed a trace which led to the Bluffs on Cumberland River—afterward Nashville. In 1783 a road was opened from Clinch River directly to that point. This was a road for horsemen and wagons, over which large numbers of settlers went into Middle Tennessee. They followed the road already described between the mountain ranges in Virginia, crossing New River at Inglis' Ferry, thence they proceeded down the East Tennessee Valley to the lower end of Clinch Mountain, and from thence the road led across the country, by way of Crab Orchard in Tennessee, to Nashville. It was by this road that the settlers in a great portion of Southwestern Kentucky came out. They followed the traveled way as far as Gallatin. Near that point they crossed the Cumberland, and made their way into Kentucky, taking up their residence in many of the Southerly counties of the State. By this route also they went to and fro in their subsequent intercourse with the Atlantic States. Public men and merchants, and persons desirous of visiting old homes and friends, made their journeys over this road on horse-back or in vehicles, or on foot, until the beginning of steam navigation on the Western rivers.

This route appears to have been suitable for carriages and wagons from the time it was first opened. The country through which it led was less wild and rough than that in Kentucky traversed by the Wilderness Road, yet the difficulty of travel from East Tennessee to Nashville is graphically described in a speech in the United States Senate, by Mr. Mason, of Virginia, in 1802. He says the traveler

"Will have to pass through the country of the Cherokee Indians, nearly one hundred miles over the Cumberland Mountains, where he will be exposed to every inclemency of the weather without a shelter to retire to, for there is not a house nor a hut in the whole journey; a journey in which all travelers are obliged at all times and of unavoidable necessity to sleep *one* night at *least,* and from the fall of rains and rise of water-courses often many nights, without a roof to cover them from the beating of the storm, and moreover where they are liable at every step to be robbed by the Indians, as I myself experienced passing through that wilderness."

Mail Facilities.

One of the privations of the early settlers resulted from the difficulty of communicating by letter with friends and kindred from whom they had parted. The means of transmission of letters was by the hand of some one going or returning. It became a custom to advertise the time and place persons would start on a trip to the States, in order that they might be the bearers of letters and messages. One of the most interesting things connected with the early days in Kentucky was the Kentucky Gazette, a paper published at Lexington, by John Bradford, beginning in 1787. Almost every issue of that paper contained a notice of a proposed trip to the East. The following is a copy of one of these notices: "A large company will start from the Crab Orchard on the 20th of Feb. in order to go through the Wilderness." These notices are very suggestive. They bring vividly before the mind that there were dangers to be guarded against by traveling in large companies. They suggest the interest that would attach to the gathering of such a company; the eagerness with which letters would be prepared, and the distances they would be carried to have them go with the company. Those who were to make the journey were leaving loved ones in the dangers of the wilderness. Swift and cruel death might come to one or the other before they ever again met. The arrival of travelers from Kentucky would be hailed in the East, and who can picture the joy attending their return again, bringing intelligence from the old homes in the East to the new ones in the West.

The files of the Kentucky Gazette show that in 1793 Jacob Meyers, a man of enterprise and public spirit, advertised that he would carry letters from Limestone to Pittsburgh by the river. At this date Indian outrages were largely abated. Yet it appears from his advertisements that danger was still apprehended. The following is taken from the Kentucky Gazette:

Armed sailing and rowing boat, to go up and down the Ohio River between Pittsburg and Limestone, which will be used as a convoy to other boats, and also to convey passengers, letters, etc., to the places above mentioned. The above boat will be completed by the 15th of Oct. * * * *. Jacob Meyers, Pittsburg, Sept. 10, 1793.

Another advertisement similar to this is given in Collins' Kentucky, vol. 2, page 113.

In 1794, Kentucky being then one of the States of the Federal Union, received mention in the Act of Congress to establish Post-offices and Post-roads. By that Act the following routes were established:

"From Philadelphia by Lancaster, Yorktown, Carlisle,

Shippensburg, Bedford, and Greensburg to Pittsburg; from Pittsburg by Washington in Pennsylvania, West Liberty in Virginia, and Wheeling on the Ohio to Limestone on the Ohio, and Fort Washington; from Limestone by Bourbontown (Paris), Lexington, Frankfort, and Harrodsburg, to Danville in Kentucky. From Danville by Bardstown to Louisville."

It will be observed that the United States Mail for Louisville left the river at Limestone, and went by way of Danville! This serves to illustrate what has been already shown that at that date overland travel was preferred to travel by the river.

The following extract from a letter from Hon. John Brown to Harry Innis, found among the Innis papers, is interesting on this point:

"PHILADELPHIA, May —, 1798.

"*My Dear Sir:* I have lately had the pleasure to receive several letters from you which should have been acknowledged at an earlier day, but meeting with no private conveyance I declined writing by the mail, knowing the obstruction which had taken place in that channel of communication. Last December I found the contract for the carriage of the mail on the Ohio had been suspended for the winter by the Postmaster General. The Act appeared so unwarrantable that I strongly remonstrated against it. He assured me that the contract should be revived as soon as the state of the river would admit, and that he should direct the mail to and from Kentucky in the meantime to be forwarded on the Wilderness route, which would answer every purpose. But in a short time it was discovered that the communication on that route was also suspended by a defect in the arrangement which could not be remedied until a new contract, which was to commence in April, should take effect.

"In this way has the intercourse between this place and Kentucky been almost entirely cut off. Since December last, I believe not more than two mails from that country have reached this place. The Postmaster General now informs me that his arrangements for the transportation of the Western mails are complete, and that in future it will go, as well on the Ohio as on the Wilderness route, with regularity and unusual dispatch."

Another letter from Brown to Innis, dated July 10, 1790, shows that then letters were sent to Kentucky both by river and through the wilderness. He says:

" As I send this thro the Wilderness, the mode of conveyance prevents the pleasure of inclosing you newspapers, etc. Nothing in them but abuse of Congress for change of residence and tardy proceedings.

* * * * * * * * * * * * *

" If my letters had found a safe passage to Kentucky your friendly advice would have been unnecessary. I have written many to my friends in different parts of the district. My friend at Pittsburgh, who forwards my letters, informs me that many of them have certainly been lost—having sent them by Mr. May and in other boats which had fallen into the hands of the Indians. A large packet forwarded by a gentleman on his way for that country was a few days ago returned, he having declined the journey after proceeding as far as Eaton."

Names.

It is to be regretted that the early settlers, being intent only upon the business of occupying the country, and being filled with a rancorous antipathy to the Indians, gave names to the places they discovered destitute of beauty, romance or poetry. The musical Indian names found in the North, and Northwest, and in the South, are almost unknown in Kentucky. One reason for this is found in the fact already mentioned, that Kentucky was not the residence of the Indians, but was only a hunting ground. The name Kentucky is an exception, so also is Ohio, but the exceptions are few. Opposite the mouth of Scioto River there was an Indian town, and the locality retains the name Indian Fort. The little stream upon which Richmond, Ky., is situated is called Town Creek—"owing to an old Indian town near where the court-house stands, observed in 1775." Such is the testimony of Archie Woods in a deposition filed in the Madison Circuit Court.

The name "Dreaming Creek," in Madison County suggests an exception to the unpoetical character of pioneer nomenclature. But the origin is this, Daniel Boone while asleep on its bank dreamed he was stung by yellow-jackets. He interpreted the dream to mean he was to be wounded by the Indians. Shortly afterward he was wounded, and he called the stream Dreaming Creek.

The first adventurers gave such names as were suggested by natural objects, and by important or trivial events. The name Cumberland, however, perpetuates in the everlasting mountain range, and in the beautiful river, one hoary with antiquity. It came down to the Duke of Cumberland through the Cumbrians of the British Isles—the Cymry of the continent, and the Cimmerians about the Black Sea—directly from Gomer the son of Japhet. The Duke of Cumberland was a distinguished character when Dr. Thomas Walker planted the name imperishably in the West. He was the son of George II, and commander in chief of the British armies at the time troops were sent over from England under Braddock to aid the colonists in the French and Indian wars.

It is an interesting fact that the early settlers affixed the name of *Wild Crab Apple* to three different localities in the Western wilds. A place called "Crab Orchard" is found in Kentucky, Virginia, and Tennessee. There is a pleasant touch of human nature in this name. The pioneers could not comfort themselves with the apples to any great extent, but the delicious fragrance of the bloom appears to have induced settlements where the wild orchards or groves of the crab tree were found.

The various stations or forts which were dotted all over the level lands where the great army of immigrants spread themselves were principally named in honor of the leading pioneers. The memory of the Indian was seldom perpetuated in the name of mountain or stream, village or fort, and never in the roads and traces of the country. The great highway leading from the Cumberland Gap to the mouth of the Scioto, the *Athiamiowee* of the Indians, was called by the pioneers "*Warrior's Path;*" and the trace of the sagacious buffalo through the trackless forests, named by the Indians *Alanantowamiowee,* was called by our forefathers the "*Buffalo Path.*"

The following list of Indian names of rivers tributary to the Ohio was furnished me by Col. John Mason Brown. It is taken from the memorandum book of Col. Wm. Preston, whose name has been mentioned in connection with the settlement of Smithfield, near Inglis' Ferry. This book is dated 1795. The termination "*cepe*," "*seepe*," "*cepewe*," or "*seepwe*" is like "*sippi*" in *Mississippi*.

1. Miami Indian Names.

Ohio River, Causisipione.
Scioto River, Siotha-cepe.
Little Kanawha River, Onimgohow-cepe.
Great Kanawha River, Piquemetami.
Coal River, Walandeconi-cepe.
Elk River, Pequoni-cepe.
Paint Creek, Moscoos-cepewe.
Gauley River, Chinquetana-cepewe.
Bluestone River [New River?], Meccenekeke-cepewe.
Greenbriar River, Weotowe-cepewe.
East River, Notweo-cepewe.
Guyandot River, Lakeweketon-cepewe.
Big Sandy River, Wepepocone-cepewe.
Kentucky River, Milewakeme-cepewe.
Falls of the Ohio, Lewekeomi.
Great Kanawha (another name), Osane-cepewe.

2. Delaware Indian Names.

Ohio River, Kitono-cepe.
Great Kanawha River, or White-stone River, Keninsheka-cepe.
Scioto River, Siota-cepe.
Muskingum River, or Goose Creek, Muskingo-cepe.
Blue-stone River, or Big-stone Creek [New River?] Momongaseneka-cepe.
Greenbriar River, Onepake-cepe.
Elk River, or Walnut River, Toquemin-cepe.
Coal River, or Hill Creek, Walhonde-cepe.
East River, or Wyandot Creek, Talemoteno-cepe.
Gauley River, or Falling Creek, Toke-belloke.

Paint Creek, or Deer Creek, Ottowe-cepe.
Big Sandy River, or Big Salt Creek, Sikea-cepe.
Little Sandy River, or Little Salt Creek, Tangate-sikea-cepe.
Big Miami River, or Stone Creek, Oswene.
Little Miami River, or High-bank River, Pioquonee.
Guyandot River, or Narrow Bottom, Seconee.

Cumberland River prior to the visit of Dr. Thomas Walker in 1750, when he gave it the name it will forever retain, was called the Cherokee River. It also at one time bore the Indian name *Ouespere*, as appears from Cox's map of 1722.

Kentucky River was called *Cuttawa* and *Cuttawba* by the Indians. Also on Charlevoix's map, of 1744, it was called *Chonanono*. On Palairet's map, of 1756, the upper waters of this stream bore the name *Milleys' River*, which is evidently a remnant of the Miami name *Millewakeme*.

The Shawnee word for salt was *Nippipimmih*. This would have been a more musical appellation for the river which defeated candidates ascend than the one it bears.

The Pack-saddle.

The pack-saddle of the pioneers deserves mention. It was a rude contrivance made of the forked branch of a tree in keeping with the primitive simplicity of the times. When fastened upon a horse it became the receptacle of the goods and chattels to be transported. Thus were carried provisions for the journey and the household stuff and utensils needed to make life tolerable when the journey was ended and the place of residence selected. The fork had to have a particular shape and the branch of a tree which could be made into a saddle was an attractive object. It is related that an early preacher once paused in his Sunday sermon with his eye fixed on the top of a tree. He said: "I want to remark right here, that yonder is one of the best forks for a pack-saddle I ever saw in the woods. When services are over we will get it."

This method of carrying burdens caused the word "pack" to be used for "carry," and the misuse of the word is still common among Kentucky people.

Conclusion.

By the routes and methods of travel described, a people came to the land of Kentucky, in a movement which has no parallel in the history of immigration. The movement was not started by lust for gold, nor to escape persecution. The chief attraction was the fertile land of Kentucky. A land like the land of promise lay in the bosom of the far West. It was rich in soil, covered with stately timber, and watered by sparkling rivers, brooks, and springs. It belonged to those who would go in and possess it. Nerved by a dauntless courage the hunters and explorers marked the way, and their families became the advance guards of the aftercoming hosts. Then groups of families combining for mutual protection sought the Western country. The accounts of the desolate, inhospitable regions through which the journey lay did not deter them. The stories of Indian massacre did not terrify them. They toiled along the wilderness trace until the trace became a road. They braved the terrible savage until they in turn became a terror to the savage. They reared their forts, and stations, and block-houses along Kentucky River, Licking River, Green River, Salt River, and along all their tributaries from headwaters, to the Ohio, until their settlements became a State.

Bound together by ties of common interest, dangers, hopes, and privations, they strengthened the bonds by inter-marriage. A widely diffused kinship and endless interlacing of family connection is one of the features of Kentucky society. A natural inheritance from an ancestry which endured the hardships of immigration over the Wilderness Road, and braved the dangers of wilderness life, was a martial spirit which displayed itself in the subsequent wars of our country. Naturally, too, the ties of consanguinity which so generally united the families of the State fostered a social disposition and friendly liberality in living, which has become proverbial in the expression " Kentucky hospi-tality."

Nor were the effects of the great immigration of 1775–1795, confined to Kentucky alone. It was a movement of population. It suddenly established the power of the white man in the Western country. It pierced and broke the center of the barriers which had barred the West against occupation. It divided the Indians North from those in the South. It operated as a flank movement upon the powerful tribes which occupied the choicest parts of New York and Pennsylvania, and caused them to give way before the advance of civilization. It made the vast territory of the Northwest, then including Ohio, Indiana, and Illinois vulnerable to settlement. It opened the way to Tennessee and Alabama, and so crowded the Cherokee Indians in the mountain fastnesses of Northern Georgia, that they eventually accepted removal beyond the Mississippi.

Therefore it is not the Kentucky people alone who have reason to study with grateful interest the history of the Wilderness Road. The direct benefit of the movement which marked out the wilderness trace and trod it into a road, did not stop at Boonesboro or the Falls of the Ohio. It extended northward, southward, and westward. It sent its reflex influence back to the sea-coast States and led them all forward to possess the great empire of the West.

THE END.

www.ingramcontent.com/pod-product-compliance
Lightning Source LLC
Chambersburg PA
CBHW031133020426
42333CB00012B/363